EL DORADO

BUILDING
FACADES

BUILDING
FACADES

Faces, Figures, And
Ornamental Detail

ERNEST BURDEN

ISBN 0-07-008959-0

1 2 3 4 5 6 7 8 9 0   QKP/QKP   9 0 1 0 9 8 7 6

Jacket photography and design: Ernest Burden
Jacket art direction: Maggie Webster-Shapiro
Endpaper design: Ernest Burden
Book design and mechanicals: Ernest Burden
Editor: Wendy Lochner
Production: Tom Kowalczyk / Roger Kasunic

ACKNOWLEDGMENTS

This book project spans more than a thirty year period, and has had numerous advances and setbacks since the original photographic portfolio *FACADE: The Changing Face of a City* was prepared and presented to publishers in 1960. It was shunned by all local publishers who were well aware of the urban renewal controversy. The head of the local redevelopment agency offered to publish it, under the guise that they were doing the right thing. That did not appeal to me. It received only minimal attention from national publishers, who did not want to take on a local issue at that time. In 1976, the National Trust for Historic Preservation offered to include the material in their second quarterly magazine *Historic Preservation.*

The book project remained dormant for nearly twenty years. In the interim, additional photographs were taken of projects around the country, and historic structures around the world, to give it the global message it deserved. The material was presented again to publishers in the format published herein.

Throughout this long journey, there were only a handful of people involved with the project. The first is my longtime friend, Fred Stitt, who prepared the words that accompanied the original photographic portfolio. The second is my editor, Wendy Lochner, who was attracted to the expanded proposal and signed it up, not only once, but twice. It was her encouragement that kept it alive, and her editing skills that kept it moving through the final production. Finally, I owe a lot to Joy Arnold, who trudged along with me through many cities around the country and in Europe, in search of the perfect face and figure. Some of her pictures are in this book. I also appreciate her patience and understanding in seeing this project through to completion.

I want to thank all those architectural firms who supplied case study projects for the renovation and renewal sections of the book. The projects are listed in the Design and Photo Credits section at the end of the book.

Faces, figures and ornamental detail have been integrated into building forms that go back to the dawn of civilization. They once adorned every building and public plaza. They humanized the architecture. They did not originate in America, yet they were imported from the temples and palaces of Europe by the many architects who studied at the Ecole des Beaux-Arts, and replicated these forms on their buildings in this country.

Through expansion and settlement of this country, these faces and figures spread from coast to coast. Railroad terminals expanded the horizons, and wherever development went, the faces, figures and ornamental details went also. The desire to humanize the facades of buildings continued the trend for over a century beyond colonization.

There are now thousands of faces and figures on the facades of urban buildings nationwide. Most of them go unnoticed to the casual observer, since they are located above the street level. They have been looking down from their lofty positions for centuries. They are brought closer through powerful telephoto lenses.

The preservation, restoration and continued use of the structures on which these elements appear is a critical factor in our efforts to keep our architectural heritage. It is now a recognized and accepted fact that these structures are extremely valuable and well worth the investments that municipalities are now making to ensure their continued existence.

This was not always the case. It was only thirty years ago that the preservation movement truly began. The idea for this book arose as a result of two demolition decisions. The first was the wanton destruction of San Francisco Victorian buildings that stood in the path of a major urban-renewal redevelopment. While the buildings were being destroyed, I was preserving them photographically. While taking photos of this destruction, I became involved in the preservation of a building by salvaging the redwood roof of a Gothic church slated for demolition. The second project involved a building I was also preserving photographically, which was headed for ruin on its own. It was the Palace of Fine Arts, designed by Bernard Maybeck as a temporary structure for the 1915 Pan-Pacific International Exposition. The photographs of this once grand building were published in my first book. The Palace was saved from ruin by the actions of the community, the city of San Francisco, and the generous donation of a private citizen. The dichotomy that existed between these two projects caused an increased awareness for the need to preserve our architectural heritage. No one wrote any books about the buildings that replaced the Victorians, but many did write about the ones that were spared, repaired, and rejuvenated with resplendent color.

On the East Coast much older and more permanent structures were less likely to be torn down in the path of urban renewal, yet large buildings were torn down to make way for even larger ones. The demolition of New York's Pennsylvania Station in the 1960s is often considered the birth of the preservation initiative. As renovation activity gained momentum in the 1970s, the emphasis shifted from strict historic preservation to rehabilitation of older structures. Today, any building over ten years old is a target for renovation if it is to remain competitive with newer space. The curtainwall buildings that we once called modern are now beginning to fall apart, and they do not make very good ruins.

The major projects throughout the country that have recently been saved from demolition are evidence that restoration, rehabilitation and adaptive reuse are now the dominant factors for an urban policy in an enlightened society.

BUILDING
FACADES

PRECEDENTS

The development of architectural styles and ornamentation is a process of continuous evolution. Architecture is always being adapted to meet the needs of people and nations in their religious, political, social, and domestic development. Each nation is reflected in its monuments, shrines, homes and public buildings. The objects we now live with were fashioned and molded by precedents which began in the Paleolithic Age, when glaciers began to recede from Northern Europe. Prehistoric art was not meant as recordings of the era, but as ritualistic representations that would reassure the success of the hunt, on which their lives depended. There is evidence that these drawings were not spontaneous; rather, they were sketched out on a small scale and enlarged onto the grotto walls. Their location deep within the caves of Spain and France, away from the elements, accounts for their timeless preservation.

The painting, sculpture and architecture of Ancient Egypt remained unchanged for thousands of years. The architecture is characterized by massive walls and sturdy columns carrying stone lintels which support a flat roof. The Egyptians used sketch pads made of limestone chips before carvings were made on capitals, or before columns were incised with hieroglyphics. The temple was a sanctuary for the elite priesthood and kingdom and not for worship by the common people.

The architecture of western Asia equally reflects national characteristics. The Babylonians built huge terraced temples and artificial mountains in fear of their gods, and from the summit astrologer priests consulted the heavens. The Assyrians built terraced palaces on elevated platforms decorated with mural sculptures of hunting, fishing, and ceremonies. These forms exerted influence to the East in Persia, India and China, and to the western Mediterranean region. Greek art, already widespread, became the style throughout the East.

The architecture of Greece reflected a high artistic aspiration. Greek temples were public monuments. Greek national games and festivals encouraged public participation, and buildings had open colonnades, entablatures and sculptured pediments in full public view.

The architecture of Rome combined numerous elements into a homogeneous whole. The Romans brought architecture to a high state of development and sculpture to a high degree of perfection, assisted of course by Greek artists. In addition to the many stately temples adorned with fine sculpture there were many buildings designed for public purposes, such as basilicas and amphitheaters for contests between men and beasts. Roman roads, aqueducts, and triumphal arches in parts of Europe are permanent expressions of Roman power and domination, while the great baths are evidence of the luxury which contributed to the decline of the empire. The use of concrete as a building material meant that they were not limited to local materials in lands far from home, and thus Roman architecture was reproduced in all parts of Europe.

Similar movements spread through other parts of the ancient world. One occurred in Pre-Columbian Mexico; another in India and China. In Mexico, religious buildings were the most important structures and great truncated pyramids were built by the Mayans, Toltecs, and Aztecs. They were built of sun-dried brick and faced with stone slabs, sometimes richly carved in low relief or coated with lime plaster and painted. Stone surfaces were carved in intricate designs, often incorporating formalized representations of warriors, serpents, tigers, and eagles.

The civilization of India dates back only to a few hundred years B.C., according to archaeological discoveries. The primary religions, Buddhism and Hinduism are not congregational, and the earlier shrines were places of pilgrimage. It is therefore an architecture to move through and around.

The Chinese culture dates back to the twenty third century B.C., but there are no examples of architectural ornament created prior to the thirteenth century A.D. The Chinese culture spread to the east and south to the Japanese, whose art was highly individualistic. The Japanese adhered to their traditional architectural models by rebuilding them over and over in the same form for centuries.

Muslim domination began in Arabia. Details of their ornament, such as striped facades and the pointed arch, were transported by the Crusaders into other parts of Europe and found their way into the Byzantine style in Venice, Pisa, Genoa and into Spain.

The fall of Rome and the emergence of Christianity changed the look of ornamentation forever. A new direction was given to architecture as the church seat moved east to Byzantium, and the Early Christian and Byzantine style evolved for all religious buildings. The style which emerged from the Byzantine had its roots in early Roman architecture, and was called Romanesque.

It was not until architecture was designed by priests and monks that a new style developed. In the beginning it was crude, but contained all the essential elements that later developed into the refined forms of the Gothic style. It spread rapidly throughout all of Europe. It was a combination of abstract ideas and intense emotional mysticism, which made the Gothic the favored religious style. A new method of construction came about, using small stones held together in arched forms by gravity forces. The roofs were now held in position by buttresses, and weighted by pinnacles which took the thrust of the loads. Walls were no longer needed to support the roof, and became a fill-in. They could be replaced with large expanses of windows of stained glass set into carved stone frames. The scenes depicted were religious history, chronicles of kings and nobles, and events of commoners. In England decorative figure sculpture was not freely used, whereas in Belgium the facades are richly adorned. In Italy the Gothic was mixed with Romanesque and Byzantine forms as well. At the same time, feudal Europe was building fortified towns and castles.

The Renaissance had its birth in Florence and was derived from many sources of inspiration. The invention of printing aided in the dissemination of new ideas. The New World was being explored. In Italy the style was a return to the classical inventions. In France it was a transitional style from the Gothic, and used more for palaces and chateaus. German architects resisted the movement for a long time, being tied to their favorite Gothic, with excessive fanciful and grotesque sculpture. In Belgium the style did not develop to the same standard as the Gothic, and it was slow to enter the Scandinavian countries. In Russia it was difficult to escape the oriental influence already established. In England it became the style of Queen Elizabeth, where it took her name. It was a transition style from the Tudor and was used mainly for castles and country homes. In France the new style was grafted onto their native Gothic in palaces and country houses, rather than on churches. In the Netherlands it became a new style. In Spain, the style was added to the richness and intricacy of their adopted Moorish style.

The term Baroque applies to the forms of the later Renaissance. The ornament is entirely independent from the structure. Lines run in free curves, and symmetry is avoided. It flourished in France, Germany and England, but was rarely used in Italy or the Netherlands. The style later became known as the Empire Style under Napoleon. In England the Palladian style remained popular, while in Germany the revival style of Karl Friedrich Schinkel exerted enormous influence.

Publications of early theorists, such as Vitruvius, Serlio, Vignola and Palladio became copybook standards which were universally adopted and led to the Revival Style. This style was finally introduced into Germany following the Thirty Years War, and found expression in Munich, Dresden, Berlin, and in Vienna Austria. The influence of Louis XIV in France also led to a popular style. Though much of this architecture was dull, extravagantly ornate, coarse or downright ugly, there were some notable examples. Old styles were revived from time to time, and nearly every style had been around the cycle at least once.

The French adhered to classicism in part due to their unique system of art and architectural education. Winners of the Prix de Rome Competition rounded off their training by a period of study at the Academy in Rome. The architectural designs and the archaeological drawings made by the Ecole des Beaux-Arts students were widely published and had a profound influence in France and other countries.

The Victorian Style came into England as a result of the writings of John Ruskin in the *Stones Of Venice* in 1851. In the same year Viollet-le-Duc published the first of ten books on the Gothic period. Architects seized upon these publications, and developed the Victorian Gothic Style.

The most momentous developments were made in response to the industrial revolution, which produced a new set of building materials, such as iron and glass for utilitarian functions. These machine-age materials eventually took their place in the design cycle, but unadorned structural ironwork was not considered admissible. The Arts and Crafts Movement introduced ways to express new forms and led to the freedom from past styles as expressed in the Art Nouveau movement.

Art Nouveau was characterized principally by the flowing and sinuous naturalistic ornament at corners of openings or junctions of architectural features. Curvilinear motifs abounded. This linear quality was well suited to metal buildings, and a number of department stores were constructed as well as arcades, pavilions and kiosks. The style was expressed in domestic architecture through ceramic tile, frescoes, and ironwork on balcony grilles and railings. Art Nouveau may have been excluded from the mainstream of history because some called it a decorative art. It was eventually rejected by the avant-garde and never became a style to be imitated, partially because it was so individualistic, yet its influence can still be felt in our own century. There was also a direct link between the style and futurism, and it profoundly affected notable imaginative architects in America, particularly Louis Sullivan.

Louis Sullivan defined the principles of organic architecture, later expanded upon by Frank Lloyd Wright and Bruce Goff. An organic building was the outgrowth of an expression of the building's function and the honest use of materials. In natural organisms there is a harmony between the parts in relation to the whole, and this became the hallmark of the organic approach to the design of a structure.

The architecture of a new country has an intimate connection to the style of the country of origin of the artist or architect. Styles of almost all the European countries were represented in America. The architecture of New England followed the pattern of English heavy-timber prototypes, while in Virginia the Georgian style, copied from English models, was most prevalent. After a while they became united into a Colonial Style. In Latin America the colonial style shows derivation from Spanish and Portuguese models, and Moorish influence is apparent. There were other examples of Spanish and French Renaissance and Baroque. This was a popular style for the elaborate movie palaces constructed in major cities across America. These revival styles predominated for almost a century, and early American architects built significant work in the Gothic and Romanesque vernacular. Eventually, American architects broke with tradition, and coupled with the influx of talented architects fleeing European domination developed a new modern design vocabulary.

The use of flat geometric shapes may have had its roots as far back as Crete or Mycenae, Egypt or Mexico, all uncovered by archaeological findings. When these were combined with those developed by the Arts and Crafts Movement and Secessionists of Europe, the Moderne or Art Deco style was the result. A wide variety of geometric forms were adopted to cinemas, shops, hotels, restaurants and ocean liners. This style exhibited a lively abstract decorative quality with a love for sensuous textures and exquisitely applied architectural ornament and abstract geometric detail. Another influence was the evolving modes of travel and communication, such as the radio, telephone, automobile, ocean liner and airplane. The style was theatrical, romantic, streamlined, sculptural, and filled with fantasy and animation.

A movement in the early part of the twentieth century led aesthetic reformers to reject ornament as clutter, and even spoke of it as a crime. In Europe, rectilinear cubistic designs known as the International Style dominated the scene. Reconstruction efforts all over Europe gave architects the opportunity to work on domestic architectural projects on a grand scale. Large scale apartment complexes were built, even entire cities. The influence of the International Style was widespread. Forms were freer, but practical functional considerations were paramount. The use of reinforced concrete produced sculptural forms that were expressive of a newfound structural freedom.

In the twentieth century ornament virtually disappeared. It was deliberately excluded from new buildings. Efforts at ornamentation were continued solely by the manipulation of construction elements, and by the exploration of the color and texture of materials, such as marble, bronze and tinted glass. Steel framing gave buildings self-sufficient strength, allowing thin skins to be developed. Ornamental patterns were used in glazed brick, molded sheet metal, glass panels, pierced screens in metal and concrete and in exposed structural grids or "brise soleil" elements. Materials play an important part in Postmodern structures, and the combination of forms call upon some of the abstract qualities of past eras.

One can trace this metamorphosis of architectural style, form and ornamentation in the pages of the following chapter. The projects are arranged chronologically to assist in following the development of these styles, and to give the flavor for the architecture of an era, or for a building that was designed in a particular architectural style.

The isolated culture of Egypt, along the Nile River, was ruled by an authoritarian priesthood and monarchy. Their beliefs are preserved in bas-relief carvings, paintings and sculptures that decorate tombs, monuments and temples. Visually, the scale of the architecture provides drama and impact. The impressive pyramids and sphinx at Giza and the great rock-cut tomb at Abu Simbel, where giant figures were carved out of the mountain, are characteristic examples.

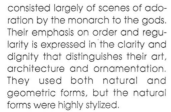

4

consisted largely of scenes of adoration by the monarch to the gods. Their emphasis on order and regularity is expressed in the clarity and dignity that distinguishes their art, architecture and ornamentation. They used both natural and geometric forms, but the natural forms were highly stylized.

Temple walls were immensely thick and sloped inwards towards the top, carved with stylized figures and symbols throughout. The walls were first chiseled smooth and the figures were drawn with a red outline. The sculptor then chiseled the forms into the stone in low relief. The decoration of temple walls

Columns were heavy and elaborated with painting and low-relief carving. There were many varieties of columns with distinctly ornate capitals based on the lotus flower, papyrus bundle, or palm. To the Egyptians, the temple signified the world: the ceiling was the heavens, under which the columns, made to represent plants, rose up to support it. All the carved elements on the temples were highly symbolic. The vulture with outspread wings symbolized protection. The scarab, or sacred beetle, was symbolic of creation and life. The sphinx, or reclining lion with a human head, symbolized divine power.

Human figures were usually shown with the head in profile. At times the middle body appeared in a frontal view and the legs and feet in profile. The same clarity of style and sophistication of form were maintained for centuries, and influenced many other civilizations. There is no other civilization where art, architecture, religion and social life were integrated into one expression. Many of these components were later transformed and refined by the Greeks and Romans. The spread of the Roman Empire eventually supplanted the Egyptian art forms, and they were never again repeated.

MESOPOTAMIA

A civilization developed along the Tigris and Euphrates Rivers at about the same age in antiquity as Egypt. The characteristic material for building was air-dried brick. Walls were covered with glazed terra-cotta representing animals and human forms. The external walls were plainly treated, but ornamented with relief sculpture of polychrome brick. Doorways were spanned by semicircular arches, ornamented with glazed brick around the edges.

The Palace of Darius at Persepolis is organized within a rigid grid on a raised platform. The great stair leads up to the entrance gates flanked by winged bulls with human heads, built partially into the walls. Mural decorations consisted of polychrome bricks and low-relief carvings. Columns were used extensively, widely spaced and comparatively slender since they only had to support timber and clay tile roofs. The form of the topmost part was fashioned with the head of twin bulls or humans. Their writings were incised into the clay and can be found in horizontal bands of surface ornamentation at eye level.

Prehistoric Greek ornament contains many Egyptian and Assyrian motifs. Greek architecture was derived from wooden structures, and the forms carried over into stone ornament. Not only did the structure become a standard "kit of parts" at a very early date, but the detailing was rigidly determined within three distinct systems, known as the Orders. The Doric and Ionic were the earliest, followed by the Corinthian, the most common during the Roman period.

A purity of form was characteristic of the early Doric and Ionic periods. Temples were one story high, and columns made up the entire external height. The Parthenon at the Acropolis in Athens, (447 B.C.) is the finest example of the Doric, while the Erechtheion, completed in 400 B.C., is the most notable example of the Ionic style. The unique feature of this temple is found on the "porch of the maidens." Six carved figures of draped females, or "Caryatids," were used in place of columns to support the entablature. The outer leg of each figure at the corner is straight, signifying the weight supported by it.

Moldings made strong definitions in this sunny climate. and were extremely refined and delicate in contour. The acanthus leaf and scroll play an important part in the ornamentation, as did the vine and some animal forms. Greek sculpture, which has never been excelled, includes that found in friezes, tympana of pediments, acroteria, sculpted metopes, reliefs, caryatids, figure sculpture, and free standing statuary of groups, single figures and horse-drawn chariots. Color was used extensively. In many cases a specially prepared stucco was made from powdered marble dust as a base for painting.

ROME

Most Roman ornament had its base in Etruscan art, which was influenced by Greek and Persian motifs. Numerous elements were combined into a homogeneous whole, thus bringing architecture to a high state of development and sculpture to a high state of perfection. The Romans were great constructors, using concrete for their vast structures. Roman architecture was eventually entirely overgrown with ornamental additions, losing the harmony of the earlier models.

Since most early Roman structures have vanished, their design and ornamentation have been re-created year after year by students from the Ecole des Beaux Arts in Paris. The annual exhibition of work featured elaborately rendered reconstructions of Roman ruins. These included temples and public buildings with ornamental detail and sculpture. The acanthus leaf and scroll was a typical ornamental motif. Birds, reptiles, Cupids and griffins were often intertwined with this foliage. Animal forms were used in abundance. The skulls of oxen connected with garlands was one of the most popular motifs.

Aztec. Mayan and Inca architecture is radically different from anything that evolved in other civilizations. The buildings that survived are monumental in form. They consist mainly of stepped pyramidal forms with central stairways to the summit temple. New pyramids were often constructed directly over existing ones, as excavations have uncovered up to three such layers of buildings. Originally these structures were intricately carved and painted in bright colors.

The extremely stylized representation of human figures, gods, animals and vegetation on the carved walls of temples and palaces have no parallel anywhere. The sun god Quetzalcoatl was a predominant figure, shown as a feathered serpent. The highly textured horizontal facades at the site of Uxmal all have heavily ornamented friezes composed of small decorative blocks. Limestone was the main building material and was easily carved. These details and the monumental forms of this architecture inspired and influenced many modern architects including Frank Lloyd Wright.

INDIA

The earliest religious buildings in India were Stupas; the gates of the Stupa at Sanchi are still preserved in stone, derived from earlier wooden models. The carvings show local deities and the elaborate ornamentation depicts vegetation and narrative reliefs representing Buddhist legends. They were originally covered with a thin skin of plaster and gilded or painted. Indian architecture and ornamentation show an inventiveness and creative originality.

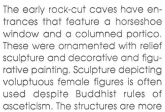

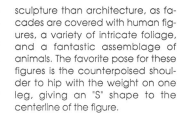

The early rock-cut caves have entrances that feature a horseshoe window and a columned portico. These were ornamented with relief sculpture and decorative and figurative painting. Sculpture depicting voluptuous female figures is often used despite Buddhist rules of asceticism. The structures are more sculpture than architecture, as facades are covered with human figures, a variety of intricate foliage, and a fantastic assemblage of animals. The favorite pose for these figures is the counterpoised shoulder to hip with the weight on one leg, giving an "S" shape to the centerline of the figure.

There are nearly eighty temples in the vast complex of Khajaraho, a city that flourished in the eleventh century. The temple represents revered mountains, the dwelling-place of divinities. The exterior is composed of multiple vertical layers of cornices and staggered projections. A profusion of carvings is found within the lower layers consisting mainly of gods in erotic poses with female divine celestial beings. Jain temples are also elaborately carved. The actual carving of the sculpture by artists was an act of worship in itself. In Hindu temples, the decoration is so lavish that columns lose their identity and become free-standing sculpture.

The Sun temple at Konarak has survived many tribulations since it was built in the thirteenth century, is now filled with sand to prevent further collapse. The temple represented a gigantic triumphal cart. The wheels at the base not only represent the chariot wheels, but was a sacred symbol of the sun, whose daily course is analogous to the course of divine law. The wheels are carved with a lacy ornate pattern, and the spokes feature carved images of dancers, voluptuous nymphs and griffins. The entire tiered pyramid is covered with sculptural figures depicting explicit and highly erotic scenes.

The architecture of Cambodia is rich in ornamental detail and characterized by it's regularity. The structures at Angkor Wat are characteristic examples. The forms rise from the jungle as a vast temple mausoleum that was designed to represent the elements of the universe. When viewed from the main entrance, the profile of the towers resemble lotus buds ready to open. The main gate leads to a great gallery richly carved with reliefs. A stairway leads up to a turreted pyramid of the innermost shrine. It was erected from blocks of plain stone and then carved in place on every surface, including parts of the roof. The galleried cloisters are filled with delicately carved bas-reliefs, illustrating scenes of Hindu mythology.

Another site where the facades are carved with extremely delicate detail is Banteay Srei. Sculptured relief figures are set into deep niches flanking the entrances from the courtyard. Ornamental carvings frame the niches. Outside the entrances are several free-standing statues, "guardian spirits." The sculptors made every effort to carve each element on the structure uniquely and the overall repetition of ornamental details provides the unifying context to the structure. These sites are among the most striking examples of the integration of sculpture and architecture that exist.

Modern craftspeople in the area have developed great skills in imitating the old styles for the purposes of restoration and development. Restoration work was begun in 1986 and has caused much debate among conservationists worldwide about the materials and methods being used. The team claims they are removing vegetation while carefully rebuilding collapsed stone. Critics maintain that the cleaning methods are abrasively scrubbing detail off the statuary and carvings, and that unskilled laborers are carelessly pouring cement into a structure originally built without mortar.

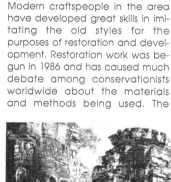

The plan of the complex at Angkor Thom features a central chapel complemented by twelve chapels radiating around it. Each tower was built over the chapels and was carved with four faces symbolizing the gaze of Buddha towards the cardinal points. The colossal faces on the towers served to identify the ruler who looked in all directions over the city. Unfortunately, the use of impermanent material led to the decay of these monuments, and they are being reclaimed by the vegetation of the jungle. Recent wars here left many land mines behind, making travel among the ruins very hazardous.

CHINA - JAPAN

Examples of Chinese ornamentation are mostly made of wood, including columns, brackets, and beams. The columns are without capitals, using tenons to connect them to beams, and the woodwork is painted with lacquer in elaborate geometric designs. The roof was a chief feature, supported on timber uprights and independent of the walls. Brightly colored glazed tiles comprise the roof, while hips are emphasized with dragons, fish, and grotesque figures.

14

A typical Japanese structure is characterized by great simplicity. Carved wooden timbers are frequently used on the gable ends of roofs and in frieze panels. The roofs are the dominant feature of this timber architecture, and exhibit a refined curvature and exotic decoration at the gable ends. They are supported on a series of compound interlocking wood brackets. Beams, brackets, carving and flat surfaces are emphasized in gilding or bright colors. Ornamental brass caps gilded for preservation are fixed to the ends of projecting timbers and over connections in wood to hide open joints.

The earliest temple form in the region of Thailand is the Lop Buri, a sanctuary formed by a stepped, pointed tower. The most famous temple in the new capital at Bangkok replaced the Khmer capital that was destroyed. It was intended to replicate the traditional style of the former temple. The Temple of the Emerald Buddha, or Wat P'ra Keo, is a temple of precious stones, formed by a sanctuary with concave roofs covered with brightly colored tiles.

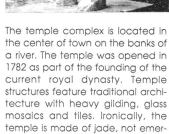

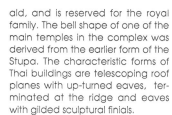

The temple complex is located in the center of town on the banks of a river. The temple was opened in 1782 as part of the founding of the current royal dynasty. Temple structures feature traditional architecture with heavy gilding, glass mosaics and tiles. Ironically, the temple is made of jade, not emerald, and is reserved for the royal family. The bell shape of one of the main temples in the complex was derived from the earlier form of the Stupa. The characteristic forms of Thai buildings are telescoping roof planes with up-turned eaves, terminated at the ridge and eaves with gilded sculptural finials.

Islam prohibited the representation of any human or animal form. This led to a conventionalized system of design in which interlacing geometrical patterns were used as background for highly decorative Arabic inscriptions. They were applied in bands and panels to exterior and interior wall surfaces and to the surface of domes. These designs were also applied to grilles in window areas to control the amount of light and to create a feeling of transparency.

The Taj Mahal at Agra, a funerary monument to the wife of Shah Jahan, is the apotheosis of the Islamic style. It carries all the motifs of earlier buildings, such as the pointed arch, which became the characteristic emblem of the style in all periods. The main building is delicately carved with tracery of abstract patterns and Islamic inscriptions incised into the marble. It has a central dome around which are four small domes at each corner. The complex is flanked by four tall minarets, set in spacious formal gardens with reflecting pools. The purity of form is heightened by the use of white marble.

St. Mark's in Venice (1063) epitomizes the Byzantine style. The glittering facade faces the piazza, which is the center of city life. The exterior was enriched by mosaics and marble decoration added during the Renaissance. It is a homogeneous blending of elements from many foreign lands. Niches and arches were each crowned by a statue. Pinnacles were added to form delicate stone frames on the facade and crowns of gold were added to the domes.

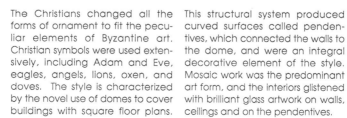

The Christians changed all the forms of ornament to fit the peculiar elements of Byzantine art. Christian symbols were used extensively, including Adam and Eve, eagles, angels, lions, oxen, and doves. The style is characterized by the novel use of domes to cover buildings with square floor plans. This structural system produced curved surfaces called pendentives, which connected the walls to the dome, and were an integral decorative element of the style. Mosaic work was the predominant art form, and the interiors glistened with brilliant glass artwork on walls, ceilings and on the pendentives.

17

PISA CATHEDRAL

The cathedral group at Pisa (1063) is one of the finest examples of the Romanesque style. Each building has a strong individuality. All three have been cleaned and restored to their original luster, revealing the delicate colors of the marble and the ornate geometric patterns of the designs. The exterior of the cathedral has bands of red and white marble, and the lower story has blind arcades. Inside the rounded arches are square designs in marble set on the diagonal.

The upper levels of the entrance facade are comprised of four tiers of arcades, one above the other. The ornamental features are delicate and refined. These columns are capped with alternating heads of humans and animals and the keystone of each arch in the arcade features a human face.

The circular baptistry (1153) exhibits extremely fine detailing in the arcade columns, which have small detached shafts. Each capital features a human head, above which is a delicate stone tracery culminating in a pinnacle or a statue. This motif is continuous around the perimeter.

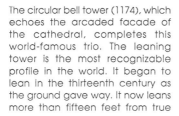

The circular bell tower (1174), which echoes the arcaded facade of the cathedral, completes this world-famous trio. The leaning tower is the most recognizable profile in the world. It began to lean in the thirteenth century as the ground gave way. It now leans more than fifteen feet from true vertical, and continues to move, despite efforts by engineers to stop it. The tower was closed to the public in 1990. Since then a girdle of steel cables was installed at the base and lead counter-weights were added on the outside. A cement ring anchors it with cables set 160 feet into the earth.

ROTHENBURG

The original town of Rothenburg, Germany was located on an elevated promontory bordered on three sides by a river. The small medieval settlement was surrounded by fortification walls, of which only the gate towers remain. The city reached its peak as an important trading center, and expanded beyond its original boundaries requiring new fortifications. Five gates control access to the city, and the wall fortifications are still in good repair.

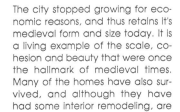

The city stopped growing for economic reasons, and thus retains it's medieval form and size today. It is a living example of the scale, cohesion and beauty that were once the hallmark of medieval times. Many of the homes have also survived, and although they have had some interior remodeling, are intact. Many have interior courtyards, but the main functions overlooked the street, and the half-timbered facades provided the ornamentation. Other devices were ornamental gable ends, most often stepped. There is constant restoration going on to maintain the town's medieval flavor.

NOTRE DAME

The masterpiece of the early French Gothic style is Notre Dame in Paris (1163). Decorative figure sculpture reached its greatest perfection in the cavernous doorways, with numerous tiers of figures in niches surrounding the arches. Corbels show carved animals, birds, and grotesques. The human figure determined the scale for statues and doorways, and they were an integral part of the structural form and thus architectural in character.

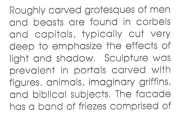

Roughly carved grotesques of men and beasts are found in corbels and capitals, typically cut very deep to emphasize the effects of light and shadow. Sculpture was prevalent in portals carved with figures, animals, imaginary griffins, and biblical subjects. The facade has a band of friezes comprised of religious figures and animals. A small replacement piece on one of the friezes shows the dramatic differences a few centuries of exposure can make on the carved stone. One of the twin towers on the main entrance facade is currently undergoing restoration and a cleaning process.

DOGE'S PALACE

The Doges Palace was started in the ninth century, rebuilt several times (1309), and completed during the Renaissance (1424). The decorative character of the facade is due largely to the arrangement of the white and rose-colored marble set in a diagonal pattern and pierced by large ornate windows. The entire facade is topped with a lacelike parapet of oriental cresting. The facade has a total length of 500 feet with open arcades on the two lower stories.

The capitals in the columns of the lower-story arcade are carved in low relief with multiple faces of animals and humans in diminutive scale. The whole scheme of columned and pointed arcades and long lines of open tracery make it uniquely Venetian Gothic. The Gothic style was a complex system composed of many ornate elements. Unity was attained by the observance of proportion, and the strict adherence to a design grid. These modules were initially derived from dimensions that relate to the human body. The architecture therefore has an innate human scale.

CA d'ORO

The history of this palace has been as rich as it's remarkable facade. The Ca d'Oro (1424) in Venice was designed for one of the cities' merchant princes by the architect who designed the Doge's Palace. It was a remodeling of an earlier Byzantine structure, and the tracery of the water gate arcade was retained in the new design. This entrance is flanked by wide arches with projecting balconies above. It is topped with ornamental cresting similar to the Doge's Palace.

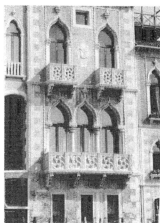

The solid wing of masonry sets off the intricate tracery of the center. The richness of the marble facing and the intricacy of the decoration is picked out with gilded details, hence the name "golden house." The building was given to the city of Venice and opened as a museum in 1927. It was restored again, and at the time of these photos was undergoing another restoration using modern technology. As the work was being completed a photographic documentation was being made of the restoration of this famous facade. The style has been copied on numerous other facades in Venice.

The Cathedral in Florence (1296) is the most prominent feature in the city, and is most notable for its multicolored marble panelings. The facade has darkened over the ages and is currently being restored to its brilliant luster. Several notable architects worked on the designs: the final dome was added by Brunelleschi. Circular windows on the drum of the dome are repeated along the facade, and a large window with delicate tracery appears over the main entrance.

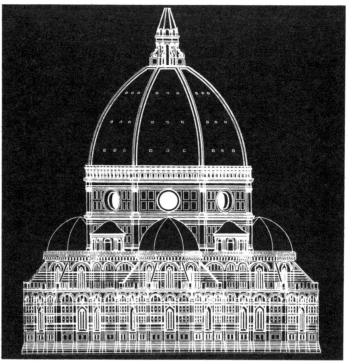

The Campanile, designed along traditional lines by Giotto (1334), was changed twice during its construction. All sides of the bell tower are paneled in the same green, pink, and white marble as the Cathedral in precise geometric patterns. The top section of the belfry is crowned by an arched corbel table. The Baptistry is a smaller octagonal structure famed for its bronze doors, designed by Ghilberti, whose head appears in relief along with dignitaries of the church. The Baptistry dome was encircled by an iron chain at the base, installed by Michelangelo in view of an impending collapse.

MILAN CATHEDRAL

Milan Cathedral (1385) one of the largest medieval churches, involved so many architects and masons that the archives became a directory of architects and builders in Europe. One of those designs shows the grid that was characteristic of Gothic designs. The exterior triangular facade is a gleaming mass of white marble with lofty traceried windows, carvings and gargoyles, flying buttresses and pinnacles topped with religious statuary.

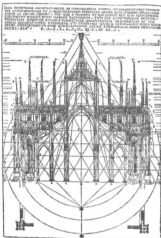

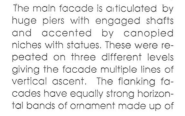

The main facade is articulated by huge piers with engaged shafts and accented by canopied niches with statues. These were repeated on three different levels giving the facade multiple lines of vertical ascent. The flanking facades have equally strong horizontal bands of ornament made up of canopied statuary and rows of gargoyles. Over the years the gleam darkened to where the sculptural detail was hardly noticeable. It is now being restored to its original luster. The scaffolding is painted the same light color as the building, thus minimizing it's intrusion upon these unique Gothic forms.

SAN MARIA NOVELLA

The Gothic church San Maria Novella in Florence (1278) was designed as a Latin cross. The original design of the exterior is indicated by blind arcades with pointed arches on the lateral facade. The pointed arches have a banded design of light and dark marble. The entrance facade was completed from designs by Alberti (1456) and added during the Renaissance. The existing doorways have pointed arches, while the new ones are rounded.

26

The same banding is used at the corners of the new facade. This motif is repeated in vertical bands around the large window and at the edges of the large scrolls. It was one of the first facades in which flanking scrolls were used to unite the two side aisles and nave into one composition. The entire facade represents a highly controlled design, and retains the honest expression of its application over the original structure by showing its thickness at the edges.

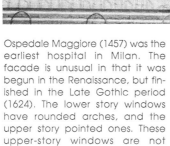

Ospedale Maggiore (1457) was the earliest hospital in Milan. The facade is unusual in that it was begun in the Renaissance, but finished in the Late Gothic period (1624). The lower story windows have rounded arches, and the upper story pointed ones. These upper-story windows are not aligned with the arcade on the bottom floor. It is built of brick and terra-cotta, which resulted in the delicacy of modeling in the broad frieze between the stories and the ornamental bands around the windows. The spandrels of the arcades have heads of people projecting out from medallions.

27

RENAISSANCE

The Renaissance, which began in fifteenth-century Florence, was a peaceful revolution in painting, sculpture and architecture, and marked an end to the domination of the arts by the church. Beauty of proportions, unity of parts, refinement of details and symmetrical arrangements were all characteristics of design. Carving is executed in harmony with classic precedents in cornices, capitals, friezes and pediments, and statuary was used frequently in piazzas.

The human figure was not the unit of scale, as in the Gothic style, either for statuary or for doorways. Modules were used often to control the design of the facade. Each part of the facade was related to a unifying element, such as the width of a column or pilaster. The use of frescos on the facade was prevalent and brought painting into complete harmony with the architecture. As sculpture, stucco decoration and fresco painting become more refined, the facades were rich without being overdone. The residential style developed by Palladio was an influence throughout all European countries.

PALAIS de LOUVRE

The work on the Palais de Louvre in Paris was actually begun in the twelfth century. Later, the old Gothic castle on its site was replaced with something more "up to date." The result was a structure extremely rich in carvings, with pediments above the windows, segmental pediments with profuse carvings and columns rather than pilasters. A museum of art and sculpture was installed within it in 1793, and it became known both as a palace and a museum.

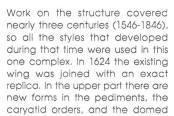

Work on the structure covered nearly three centuries (1546-1846), so all the styles that developed during that time were used in this one complex. In 1624 the existing wing was joined with an exact replica. In the upper part there are new forms in the pediments, the caryatid orders, and the domed pavilion roof. It is a curious combination of classically inspired articulation with engaged columns and enriched wall surfaces, with every variety of sculptural element to achieve greater sumptuousness. The East facade is a columned classical scheme, yet enriched with beautiful sculptured detail.

29

Baroque architecture was adapted to strict Venetian conditions, and this was beautifully expressed in the design for San Maria Della Salute (1630). The site for this church is on the entrance to the Grand Canal in Venice, the perfect setting for such a prominent structure. The architect, B. Longhena, was a stage designer. The church rises out of the water to a giant dome held up by gigantic spiral buttresses. The top of the structure is studded with statuary.

In nearly all countries the love for ornament was strong, but did not find expression until the Baroque and Rococo periods. Here ornament was brought into complete harmony with architecture, as sculpture and fresco painting become more refined. In the Baroque style ornament was larger in scale; designs were more restless and opulent. Facades were full of curves and movement, and often overdone. The style that evolved from this was the Rococo, which was similar, but smaller in scale with more delicate ornament. Many Venetian churches were designed in one or the other of these styles.

The Grand-Place is the marketplace of Brussels. It was lined with wooden houses in the twelfth century, which over time were rebuilt of stone. The various trade guilds built their meeting halls on the square and competed with each other in embellishing their headquarters in the late Belgian Baroque and Rococo fantasies. Some ornamentation is in gold leaf, which gives the facades an opulent flavor. The gabled fronts indicate the wealth of these guilds.

The entire complex was bombarded in 1700, and only a few facades were left standing. Some were restored where they stood, others were reconstructed or replaced by new buildings following plans approved by the city authorities. This is how the Grand-Place retained such harmony within the entire market square to this day. Buildings are constantly being restored and cleaned. All vehicular traffic, once traversing the square, is now prohibited.

LINDERHOF CASTLE

Ludwig II, King of Bavaria, hated crowds, preferring mountain retreats. Although he died at age forty, he had a hand in three major castle-building projects. The most famous one is the Neuschwanstein castle, built on a rock promontory. The second one, Schloss Linderhof, (1880) is in a secluded mountain area. It started out as a little garden chalet, and was expanded by an architect and stage designer from Munich. This may help explain the scale of the facades.

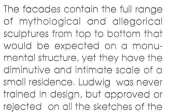

The facades contain the full range of mythological and allegorical sculptures from top to bottom that would be expected on a monumental structure, yet they have the diminutive and intimate scale of a small residence. Ludwig was never trained in design, but approved or rejected on all the sketches of the designer, even down to the last doorknob, so the results were really his own. His life was drenched in fantasy and music, and this played an important role in the design of this castle. In the front of the castle there is a large reflecting pool containing a fountain with gilded reclining statuary.

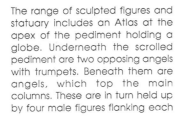

The range of sculpted figures and statuary includes an Atlas at the apex of the pediment holding a globe. Underneath the scrolled pediment are two opposing angels with trumpets. Beneath them are angels, which top the main columns. These are in turn held up by four male figures flanking each side of the entrances to the castle. On the main facade there are four niches, each containing statuary. There is additional free-standing statuary at the stairways leading to the pool containing the gilded fountain. A grotto built into the hillside contained a lake and a swan boat.

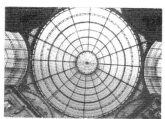

34

The Galleria Vittorio Emanuelle in Milan (1856) is an imposing structure with an iron and glass-roofed arcade. It is arranged on a cruciform plan with a domed octagon at the crossing of the barrelvaulted ceilings. The style of the interior facades is classical. This is in effect roofing over the street, wherein the exterior facades are now enclosed by a roof which admits natural light into the vast interior space. This concept of the roofed arcade originated in Brussels and was copied everywhere. The unique aspect here is the intersecting of two arcades. This is the predecessor of many modern malls.

The Castiglioni Palace in Milan (1903) is a mixture of decorative Renaissance elements and Art Nouveau motifs. The floral ornaments and the frieze of cherubs above the windows add vitality to the otherwise solid and dignified facade. At the base, windows are treated with an imaginative rustication with iron grilles set into bold and irregular stone openings. The iron grilles are similar to Art Nouveau designs, and offer a human scale to the massive facade. A later version of this design, also in Milan, echoes the continuous frieze of cherubs across the facade above the window pediments.

35

Throughout the centuries facades have been constructed either from wood, stone, brick, or marble. In the eighteenth century techniques were developed by which melted iron could be poured into molds, producing cast forms on a large scale. The use of cast iron for columns and wrought iron for beams meant that structures could be taller, due to greater strength of these materials. Methods were devised for fastening the parts and a new building form was born.

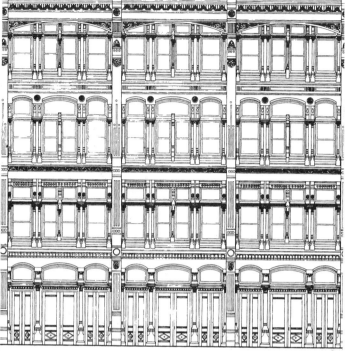

Once a wooden pattern was carved, sand molds were used to cast identical and interchangeable elements. They could be machined to a perfect fit. This was the first mass production of interchangeable elements making up a building's facade. The entire facade could be laid out on the foundry floor, much like the small stones of the Gothic cathedrals, which were first assembled on the floor before being erected. The parts would be labeled and could be transported a few blocks or shipped across the country. Many of the buildings were erected in the immediate vicinity of the foundry.

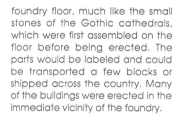

The taste for European architectural styles eventually replaced the functionalism of the original designs, at first with Renaissance and Classical forms and later with more elaborate ornamentation as the century progressed. Cast-iron facades were often textured and painted white to look like cut stone or carved marble. They were very popular for large scale retail stores in urban areas, and featured designs with stylistic ornamental features. The combination of cast-iron buildings and the passenger elevator developed in the 1870's, led eventually to the development of the modern office skyscraper.

CAST-IRON FACADES

The Gilsey Building, now demolished was among the first total iron facades in New York City. One of the cast-iron structures still standing is the Gilsey House, a flamboyant iron and marble eight-story hotel built in 1869. Across its sculptured facade the structure features coupled columns, broken pediments, urns, Palladian windows, a clock supported by a large human face and a slate mansard roof. It was recently converted into a luxury apartment building.

One of the first cast-iron facades in New York City was designed for the Singer Sewing Machine Company. At twelve stories it was the tallest building in the world in 1908. A second building for the same company was later constructed of iron, terra-cotta and glass that foretold the glass curtain wall. It was called the Little Singer Building, after its larger predecessor. The delicate balconies and tracery framing the great arch at the top is of wrought iron, not cast iron.

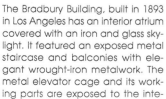

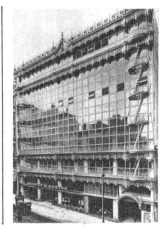

The Bradbury Building, built in 1893 in Los Angeles has an interior atrium covered with an iron and glass skylight. It featured an exposed metal staircase and balconies with elegant wrought-iron metalwork. The metal elevator cage and its working parts are exposed to the interior. It was abandoned for many years, and used as a set in the futuristic movie "Bladerunner", as a symbol of a decaying civilization. It was restored to its original condition in 1969, and is now a prestigious private office complex as well as a National Historic Landmark.

The Hallidie Building in San Francisco was designed by James Willis Polk in 1917. It was originally built as a speculative investment, yet it was prophetic of techniques that would become widely used many years later. The main facade consists of a great glass "curtain," broken only by the horizontal and vertical glazing grid. The main structural members are three feet behind and completely free from the glass wall. It is enriched at the top by bands of intricate fretted metalwork. The building became an official landmark in 1971.

CARPENTER GOTHIC

The seat of development after the 1850 Gold Rush was San Francisco, as more than sixteen thousand homes were built in the two decades that followed. Those that survived were in areas not destroyed by the 1906 earthquake and fire, or those that escaped urban renewal programs. The result of such programs can be seen in the renovation section of this book, as many of these homes were destroyed by the wrecker's ball, the impetus for producing this book.

Wooden structures were built for centuries with mortice and tenon joints. Balloon-frame construction did away with the need for such skills. Carpenters would add exotic moldings and carvings on impulse, as redwood used for ornamental details was plentiful and easy to carve. Some of the most attractive facades were the product of a carpenter's imagination, hence the term "Carpenter Gothic." Other classifications of the Victorian Style include the Italianate, Stick Style, Romanesque, Queen Anne, and Eastlake.

The details, scrolls, fretwork, fans, string courses, dentils and ornamental brackets were all designed to capture the eye with the sumptuous play of light over form. Towers, turrets and cupolas added to the basic building block as balusters, dentils, lion heads, faces of babies and young maidens, and rosettes were added to the facades. The detail worked at all levels of scale from a single building to groupings and facades of entire streets. Many of these fine houses were refurbished and given a new life through a group of local artists and painters who created the now-famous "painted ladies."

38

COMMERCIAL VICTORIAN

The Victorian Style was most popular for domestic architecture, mainly because the wooden ornamentation was suited to the residential scale, but it was a design style for commercial buildings as well. The ornamentation was ei-ther stone or metal, as fire codes were more stringent for commercial structures, and the scale of ornamentation was significantly larger. The use of bay windows was a typical device used to enhance and further articulate the facade.

Frank Furness designed this highly individualistic building in 1871 for the Pennsylvania Academy of Fine Arts in Philadelphia. The design of the facade makes imaginative use of forms from a diversity of styles. It was highlighted by a polychromatic masonry set in diagonal patterns. The ornamentation consisted of a combination of Victorian and other completely unique elements. Bas-relief sculpture was set into panels within the brickwork. At the time of this design the architect employed the young Louis Sullivan as an assistant in his office. The building has recently been restored and cleaned of years of grime.

THE ROOKERY

The Rookery in Chicago takes its name from the word "rook", a chess piece resembling a castle. The building resembles a castle with its turrets, light court, oriel staircase and arched entrance. At twelve stories high it was the tallest building in the world when it was built in 1888. In 1905 Frank Lloyd Wright updated the lower floors by re-designing the stairs, installing giant planters at the base of the main staircase, and having the marble incised with designs in gold leaf.

Years later, other architects modified the design and painted over the skylight that covered the lower floors of the light well. This was restored in 1992 to it's original translucency by preservartion architect Thomas Harboe, of McClier. The glazed white brick in the interior light court was also restored. The metal ornament framing the windows and capitals were painted gold recalling the gold leaf of the marble inside. The renovation produced an iridescent quality that contrasts with the rusticated facade. This was the most extensive restoration ever undertaken of a historic American office building.

PARLIAMENT HOUSE

This reddish-brown sandstone building is home to the Legislative Assembly of Ontario, Canada. The style of the building, built in 1896, is Victorian Romanesque. It is a robust example of the integration of sculpture and stonework. A frieze depicting allegorical figures and objects appears on the main facade between giant circular windows. It is fifteen feet high and seventy feet long. In the center of the frieze and in place of one of the windows is the provincial seal.

A multitude of unique carvings adorn the exterior facades. The vigorous carvings appear in unexpected places. Faces of humans and mythical beasts are intertwined. The heads of important people in the history of the province are carved in richly ornamental panels. At one time ivy had obliterated them, and was destroying other fragile carvings. The ivy was removed and a continuous program of maintenance has preserved the stone. Flanking the main entrance are two finely carved heads above a triple set of columns. Each resembles an animal with human characteristics.

All the elements of the modern skyscraper were developed in the Wainwright building in St. Louis, designed in 1890 by Louis Sullivan. The entire building is carried on a steel frame, fireproofed by a brick and terra-cotta sheathing. Uninterrupted columns go from above the base to the high-relief frieze which is capped by a bold cornice. In between the columns are narrow windows with ornamental terra-cotta spandrels set back from the columns to emphasize verticality.

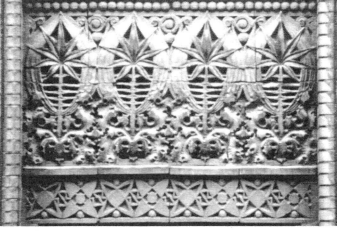

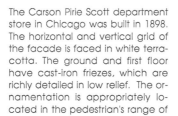

The Carson Pirie Scott department store in Chicago was built in 1898. The horizontal and vertical grid of the facade is faced in white terra-cotta. The ground and first floor have cast-iron friezes, which are richly detailed in low relief. The ornamentation is appropriately located in the pedestrian's range of vision, and it emphasized the main entrance. The glass behind the ornamental panels was originally opaque, but has been replaced with clear glass, following a recent restoration of the ornament. This unique corner is a fantasy of flowing organic forms, an imaginative example of Sullivan's ornament.

The Bayard Building, a 12-story structure designed in 1898, was Sullivan's only New York City building. It was the first to break away from the layer-cake articulation and stress its verticality in steel bearing piers and white terra-cotta spandrel panels. The ornamental spandrels were repeated throughout the height except for the top floor where lion's heads appear. Between the top arched bays are winged female figures terminating each major vertical pier.

43

The young architect Frank Lloyd Wright purchased a corner lot on a busy street connecting downtown Chicago with the western suburb of Oak Park. He built a showcase home there, and attracted many clients who built their homes in the immediate neighborhood. There were over thirty such homes when he added his architectural studio to the residence. During this time he developed his theory of "organic architecture," experimenting with many innovative ideas on his own home and studio. It is now a musuem owned by the National Trust for Historic Preservation, and attracts many devoted admirers.

At the entrance to his studio, Wright designed a set of four columns with sculpted capitals. The design was meant to symbolize the architect's profession. It features an asymmetrical floor plan raised in braille-like relief. An open book signifies learning with a tree of life at the top. The design was flanked by two storks in a frontal view. Many make the pilgrimage to this studio and tour neighboring houses, such as the Moore House located a few blocks away. Also nearby is Unity Temple, his most famous church, characterized by the simplicity of its external monolithic massing, and the sculpted ornamental detail.

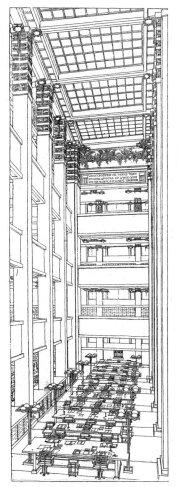

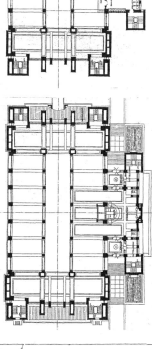

The Larkin Building of 1906 was one of the more important architectural landmarks. It was the first fully air conditioned office block on record, with a central open well of four stories. It incorporates many innovative ideas, such as the stair towers at each corner. Wright described the architecture of the times as ornamented boxes with columns in front and cornices on top. He set out to destroy the box and did so in this building. He pushed the stair towers out from the facade and broke up the walls into a series of pillars with glazing in between. It was sold to a wrecking firm in 1950 and demolished.

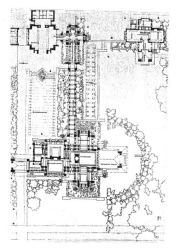

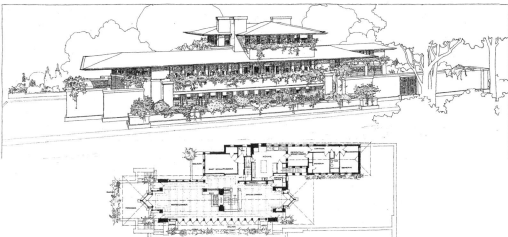

45

The concept of breaking out of the box was further explored in other residential designs, such as the D.W. Martin House and the Robie House. The concept is clearly expressed in the floor plans of these houses, where the walls are replaced with a series of piers with window or doors in between. The walls became screens and were independent of each other. The corner posts were eliminated by moving them back and cantilevering the roof planes from them, thus creating broad overhangs. The facades expressed this new kind of architecture and became much more articulated.

WEDDING TOWER

The site was prominent in the city of Darmstadt, Germany long before it was designated an artist's colony in 1889. Joseph Olbrich, leader of the colony, was asked by the Duke in 1905 to plan a tower for panoramic viewing of the town. The citizens also wanted to give the Duke a gift for his upcoming second marriage, and it thus became the Wedding Tower. It has seven levels, the fourth and fifth being reserved for the Duke and his bride and the top level was used for observation.

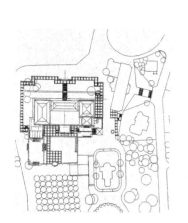

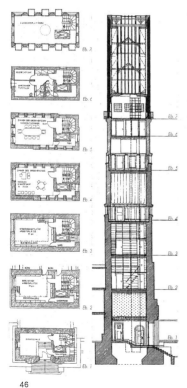

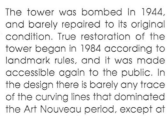

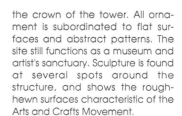

The tower was bombed In 1944, and barely repaired to its original condition. True restoration of the tower began in 1984 according to landmark rules, and it was made accessible again to the public. In the design there is barely any trace of the curving lines that dominated the Art Nouveau period, except at the crown of the tower. All ornament is subordinated to flat surfaces and abstract patterns. The site still functions as a museum and artist's sanctuary. Sculpture is found at several spots around the structure, and shows the rough-hewn surfaces characteristic of the Arts and Crafts Movement.

The unique top was popularly seen as signifying a hand raised in solemn praise. The entryway to the tower was stark and abstract. Above, a rectangular plaque shows four female figures with inscriptions describing the qualities of their leader. Power was symbolized by the lion, wisdom by the owl, justice by the scales, and mildness by an infant. Inside, the ceiling is covered with gold, and wall mosaics depict a couple in an embrace. The large sundial on the exterior features the same mosaic color scheme and is ornamented in gold, with symbols of the Zodiac appearing around the edge.

The main exhibition hall of the artists' colony at Darmstadt, also designed by Joseph Olbrich, is adjacent to the Wedding Tower. It houses individual studios, each lit by a high-sloping clerestory window. Thus there are few windows on the main facade. In front of the plain and functional facade is a lavish portal, a three-quarter circle flanked by monumental carved figures. The male figure represents strength while the female figure represents beauty.

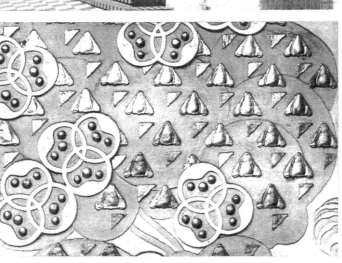

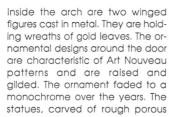

Inside the arch are two winged figures cast in metal. They are holding wreaths of gold leaves. The ornamental designs around the door are characteristic of Art Nouveau patterns and are raised and gilded. The ornament faded to a monochrome over the years. The statues, carved of rough porous stone, blackened from the elements until they were restored along with the Wedding Tower. One unique feature is the pattern of ornamental brick which flows down the entry stairs and the checkered design in the pavement, similar to the paving design at the Wedding Tower entrance.

Joseph Hoffman designed this mansion in 1905 as an asymmetrical composition in white marble. The exterior facade is extremely unified, and the forms relate to each other in simple geometric terms. It is totally free from curving arabesque lines. The tall staircase window accentuates the vertical lines of the tower. There are no moldings, yet the marble slabs are outlined like picture frames, which appear around all openings and around a panel of bas-relief figures.

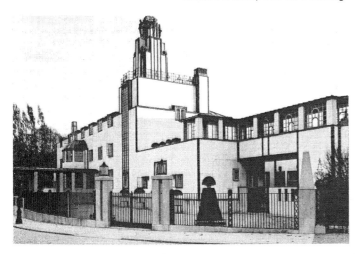  

Otto Wagner began his career by building in the historical manner, but his book *Moderne Architektur* stated a case for architecture that was free from historicism. This block of flats in Vienna (1898) has a facade ornamented at the upper level with a rich pattern. The area between the windows are designed to resemble capitals. Garlands hanging from them are accented with circular disks. Each capital has an elliptical medalion featuring the profile of a female face. Above, there are plant forms which arch over each window, connecting the medallions across the entire facade.

49

ART NOUVEAU

The Art Nouveau style is free from historicism and perfectly coherent in all its details. The typical design is based on an arabesque motif. The main materials are glass and iron. All the structural features are given ornamental values. Elevations are highly articulated, rhythmic and monumental. Striking contrasts are achieved by having sculptural members of iron support large areas of glass. Wood carvings on doorways and windows are characteristically curvilinear in form.

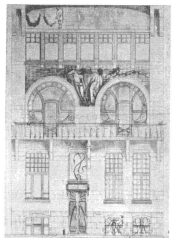

The overall character of this house designed by Paul Hankar is a combination of Late Renaissance and Art Nouveau elements. The architect showed an interest in the work of Viollet-le-Duc, yet was part of the Art Nouveau movement in Brussels. There is a mixture of ornate surface decoration with simple forms that result in an entirely modern facade. The painted fresco figures are by the owner-painter, and have faded from their original luster. Certain reference books refer to this structure as having been demolished, but these recent photos attest that it is still alive and well in Brussels.

ANTONIO GAUDI

Antonio Gaudi's work in Barcelona exhibits an organic manipulation of form which is highly original and imaginative. In the Casa Batlo the stone dressings of the lower facade are molded plastically into sinuous shapes, echoed in the upper metal balustrades, which resemble masks or skulls. The facade wall surface is studded with colored glass fragments. The roof is comprised of a sinuous undulating form of colorful tiles, capped at the ridge with overlapping round tiles.

The Casa Mila is a block of flats in Barcelona with an undulating facade enclosing polygonal rooms. The stone facade is like an eroded sea-hollowed cliff, with strap ironwork balconies that resemble seaweed riding the crest of waves.

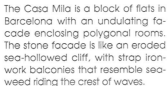

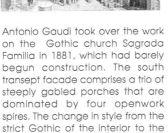

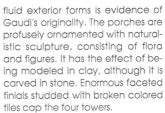

Antonio Gaudi took over the work on the Gothic church Sagrada Familia in 1881, which had barely begun construction. The south transept facade comprises a trio of steeply gabled porches that are dominated by four openwork spires. The change in style from the strict Gothic of the interior to the fluid exterior forms is evidence of Gaudi's originality. The porches are profusely ornamented with naturalistic sculpture, consisting of flora and figures. It has the effect of being modeled in clay, although it is carved in stone. Enormous faceted finials studded with broken colored tiles cap the four towers.

51

NATIONAL FARMER'S - POWESHICK BANK

Louis Sullivan's gift for innovative ornament was the outgrowth of his ideas on organic architecture. The fusion of this elaborate ornament with simple monumental forms is shown in the 1907 National Farmers' Bank in Owatonna, Minnesota. The base is red sandstone with dark red brick walls. The ornamentation is contrated in a frame of green terra-cotta with intricate cast-iron escutcheons at the corners. The main focus is provided by giant arches, one on each facade.

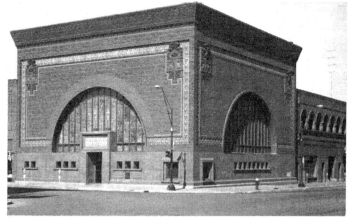

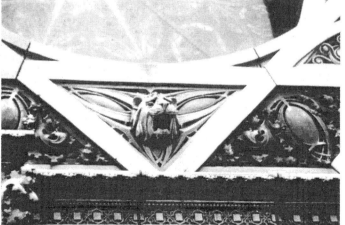

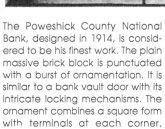

52

The Poweshick County National Bank, designed in 1914, is considered to be his finest work. The plain massive brick block is punctuated with a burst of ornamentation. It is similar to a bank vault door with its intricate locking mechanisms. The ornament combines a square form with terminals at each corner, overlapped with a square set on the diagonal with each apex ornamented. These forms encompass a circular window in the center containing a stained glass design. All the ornament is glazed terra-cotta with an interwoven design that is without precedent in American architecture.

The Peoples Federal Savings and Loan in Sidney, Ohio, was designed in 1917, and represents the maturing of Sullivan's ornamental style. There is a massive, intricately ornamented arched entry which is the main focus of the facade. Inside, the arch is a filed of colored tile, bordered by a circular band of disks. The lateral facade is equally ornate; each element is fastened to the facade with an ornamental feature. These are robust castings with naturalistic features.

The Merchants Union Bank in Columbus, Wisconsin, was his last work; designed in 1919, it represents Sullivan's most creative maturity.

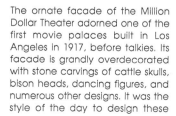

54

The ornate facade of the Million Dollar Theater adorned one of the first movie palaces built in Los Angeles in 1917, before talkies. Its facade is grandly overdecorated with stone carvings of cattle skulls, bison heads, dancing figures, and numerous other designs. It was the style of the day to design these palaces to be showplaces as entertaining as the events shown in them. Late Baroque and Rococo Revival styles were favored due to the excessive ornamentation associated with them. Many of these theaters have been threatened with demolition, while others are currently being renovated.

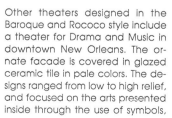

Other theaters designed in the Baroque and Rococo style include a theater for Drama and Music in downtown New Orleans. The ornate facade is covered in glazed ceramic tile in pale colors. The designs ranged from low to high relief, and focused on the arts presented inside through the use of symbols, masks, and finely sculpted figures. Another theater in the Spanish Baroque style is located in downtown Boston. However, the area around the theater is deserted, and the theater abandoned. The highly detailed design and ornamentation indicates that it was once a thriving stylish palace.

55

NEBRASKA CAPITOL

This impressive structure was designed by Bertrand Goodhue, the winner of a competition for the commission. He presented a simplified classical theme which became a prototype for much of the public architecture of the period. It was built during the Art Deco period and features a sleek staggered vertical form culminating in a dome, covered with ceramic tile. The dome was topped by a statue of a reaper, symbolic of the agricultural economy of the state.

Other western themes appear in bas-relief panels over the entrances. In one a covered wagon is pulled by oxen, above which is a frieze interspersed with ox skulls. The background of the relief is painted gold. The building contains areas of sculpture on the lower levels in panels of bas-relief carvings inset between the windows. On the corner parapets there are figures incised into the stone in such a way that they appear as an integral outgrowth of the wall surface, rather than being applied to it. All the sculptured figures and bas-reliefs represent famous historical characters in law and justice.

OMAHA UNION STATION

As the population moved west across America, railroad stations became the focus of activity in new cities. The stations were lavishly built and finished with the finest marble flooring, lighting fixtures and soaring interior spaces. President Abraham Lincoln selected Omaha as the terminus of the Union Pacific, the first transcontinental railroad. The station was designed by architect Gilbert Underwood in 1929, using monumental forms and integrated Art Deco sculpture.

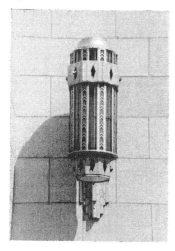

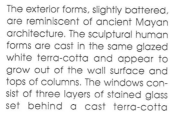

The exterior forms, slightly battered, are reminiscent of ancient Mayan architecture. The sculptural human forms are cast in the same glazed white terra-cotta and appear to grow out of the wall surface and tops of columns. The windows consist of three layers of stained glass set behind a cast terra-cotta screen. Much of the interior surface is covered with simulated marble. The Union Pacific gave the building to the city in 1973, and plans for a museum were then developed. The entire station was refurbished, and portions were redesigned into the Western Heritage Museum for the State of Nebraska.

57

One example of the infusion of classical forms with new meaning is the Liberty Memorial in Kansas City. It was designed by H. Van Buren Magonigle in 1926. It was the result of a competition patterned after the Nebraska State Capitol. It was a monument to peace, not war. The memorial's central element, a Gothic bundled shaft, is capped by a censer supported on the upstretched wings of the guardian angels, Honor, Courage, Patriotism and Sacrifice.

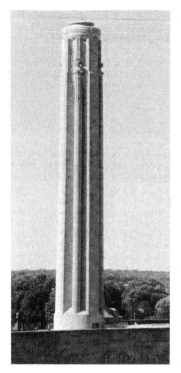

The plan was typically classical. Two sphinxes, named Memory and Future, guard the entrance to the memorial. But the sphinxes are modified with their wings raised to shield their faces, one from the horrors of war; the other from the uncertainty of the future. With this gesture, the sphinxes are stripped of explicit historical content. They are neither Egyptian nor Grecian. They do not reveal whether they are male or female, nor whether they are animal or human. It is a departure from tradition that brings a new meaning to Classical architecture, and they carry the forms of the past into the present.

GOVERNMENT BUILDINGS

The Ontario Government Building in Toronto was erected in 1926 of poured concrete. There are ornamental friezes running around the entire parapet featuring animals and naturalistic ornament. A large frieze over one entrance depicts workers' activities. Animal heads appear on medallions within the spandrels over the arched doorway. Flanking each side of the door are large stone figures. The entire building is topped with a dome of brightly colored tile.

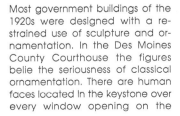
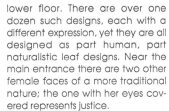

Most government buildings of the 1920s were designed with a restrained use of sculpture and ornamentation. In the Des Moines County Courthouse the figures belie the seriousness of classical ornamentation. There are human faces located in the keystone over every window opening on the lower floor. There are over one dozen such designs, each with a different expression, yet they are all designed as part human, part naturalistic leaf designs. Near the main entrance there are two other female faces of a more traditional nature; the one with her eyes covered represents justice.

ART DECO

The Boston Avenue Church in Tulsa, Oklahoma, was designed by Bruce Goff at age twenty two, when he was still apprenticed to Rush, Endicott and Rush. It reflects the Art Deco period with its stylized, elongated figures over the entry and along the roof's perimeter. Some of the figures represent founders of the Methodist church. Along the roof are metal and glass pinnacles which echoe the abstract design of the stained glass lantern at the top of the tower.

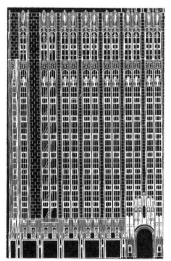 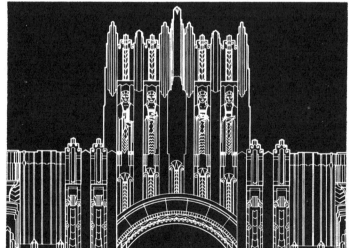 

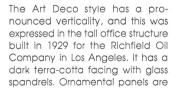

60

The Art Deco style has a pronounced verticality, and this was expressed in the tall office structure built in 1929 for the Richfield Oil Company in Los Angeles. It has a dark terra-cotta facing with glass spandrels. Ornamental panels are located on the lower level and at the parapet. The main focus of the building is at the entryway, which features Art Deco ornamentation. Four abstract figures are incorporated within the characteristic angular motifs.

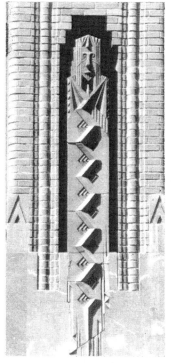

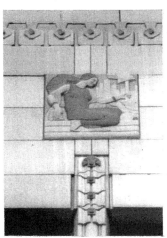

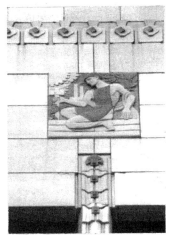

The Art Deco style draws its inspiration from Art Nouveau, Cubism, the Bauhaus and many other sources. They are all simulated in a distinctive style which emphasizes geometric patterns, hard edges, and angular compositions. Facades frequently employed bands of zigzag or chevron designs in bands or friezes. These usually run in a horizontal direction across the lower levels of the structure. Low-relief ornamentation is common around door and window openings and around parapets. Tile was a favored material because it was easily cast into geometric shapes, and glazed with bright colors.

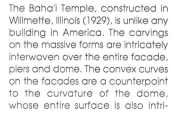

The Baha'i Temple, constructed in Willmette, Illinois (1929), is unlike any building in America. The carvings on the massive forms are intricately interwoven over the entire facade, piers and dome. The convex curves on the facades are a counterpoint to the curvature of the dome, whose entire surface is also intricately carved in arabesque designs to produce a screen through which light filters. It was originally built with a skylight under the dome. It was recently retrofitted with a new skylight over the existing one, which not only provided extra weather protection but made it more thermally efficient.

This hotel in Phoenix was designed in 1929 by Albert Chase Arthur, an apprentice to Frank Lloyd Wright. Wright was a consultant on the project and his influence is evident. Everything on the property is Wrightian, from the registration forms to the pats of butter and soap stamped with the concrete block design, to the patterned concrete blocks themselves. The design motifs throughout are inspired by Aztec Indian sites in Mexico that Wright had just visited.

This is the largest example of textile block design in the country. The architect set up a plant on the site and supervised the manufacture and installation of the blocks. Some are solid, some are patterned, and some are pierced, making the facade glow at night. The building has been renovated several times.

The last one, after a fire in 1973, departed from the original scheme, but was returned to the original in more recent restorations. The free-standing group of figures at the entryway was sculpted by Alfonso Ianelli, a friend of Wright. They were originally in the Midway Gardens in Chicago, which was demolished.

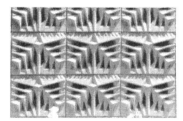

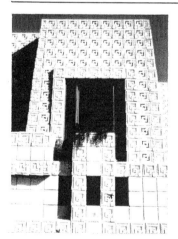

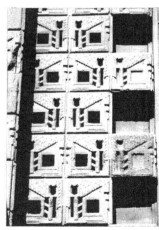

63

Among other structures that exhibit Wright's designs using patterned blocks are the Ennis House (left) and the Freeman house (right), both in Los Angeles, and the Imperial Hotel in Tokyo (center).

The patterned block in the hotel was carved fron native lava rock, rather than cast in cement as the other designs. The hotel was demolished despite international efforts to save or preserve it.

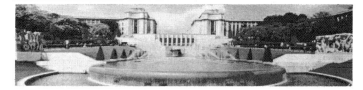

64

The Palais de Chaillot was designed in conjunction with the Museum of Modern Art for the 1937 International Exhibition in Paris. The overall layout is Beaux-Arts; a strictly symmetrical scheme of two separate but identical structures that flank an open courtyard on the axis with the Eiffel Tower. The concave arced surfaces of the corners are echoed in the layout of the plaza and fountains below. Grand staircases are terminated with immense nude stone figures, one on each side. Free-standing sculpture surrounds the building, and blocks of stone figures are displayed in the gardens below.

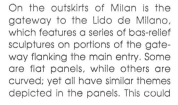

On the outskirts of Milan is the gateway to the Lido de Milano, which features a series of bas-relief sculptures on portions of the gateway flanking the main entry. Some are flat panels, while others are curved; yet all have similar themes depicted in the panels. This could be described as the "profane" side of allegorical figures as compared to the "idyllic" sculptures of the Palais de Chaillot. Here satyrs dance with female figures, some depicted as mermaids, some on horseback. Yet all appear to be having a good time.

ROCKEFELLER CENTER

The plan for this grouping of buildings was initiated in 1928 by the Metropolitan Opera of New York City. John D. Rockefeller acquired the tract of land in the middle of the city, so the project bore his name. With the crash of 1929 the opera withdrew its plans, and a tall, slim office building was designed on the site for the Radio Corporation of America by the firms Reinhard and Hofmeister; Corbett, Harrison, Macmurray; and Raymond Hood, Godly and Fouilhoux.

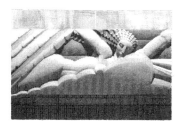

The European academic principles of the Ecole de Beaux-Arts had to be combined with a modern transportation network, shipping areas, and mechanical and electrical equipment for a modern high-rise office tower, according to New York City zoning and structural guidelines. Smaller office buildings flanking the RCA building reflected the same setbacks and stepped slab design. The horizontal moldings on the facades of these lower structures created uninterrupted perspective lines that converge like pointers at the entrance to the main focal point of the project, the RCA Building with its open plaza.

The embellishments are all in the Art Deco style and occur mainly at the street level. There was an emphasis on public spaces, and extensive bas-relief sculptures that feature human figures can be seen on the lower floors of all structures and alongside a down-ward sloping pedestrian mall, leading to a sunken plaza containing an ice rink. The eighteen-foot-high gilded statue of Prometheus, weighing eight tons, was sculpted by Paul Manship and unveiled in 1934. The figure is surrounded by a ring bearing the signs of the Zodiac representing the cosmos, while the figure delivers the stolen fire.

67

The International Building is a symbol of cooperation among nations for world peace. symbolized by the seven-ton, fifteen-foot high cast bronze statue of Atlas by sculptor Lee Lawrie. Isamu Noguchi designed the ten-ton steel relief sculpture on the main entrance to the Associated Press Building. It represents the use of the camera, telephone, wirephoto, teletype and pad and pencil in world communications. The most notable structure is Radio City Music Hall, a New York City landmark. All bas-relief sculptures on the group of structures were cleaned, painted, and gilded to a brilliant display of color.

MIAMI BEACH ART DECO

Born out of speculation and designed for fun, the Art Deco style of Miami Beach from its inception has been the result of fantasy. The original white facades were very flamboyant and enlivened with tropical pastel colors accentuating the geometric designs and patterns in the stucco exteriors. The facades were most often symmetrical, and featured stepped planes, corner windows, stripes, ornamental motifs set into panels, and abstract floral designs.

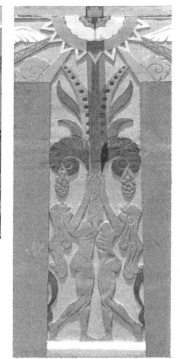

Features like corner windows were often created by the builders and displayed an inventiveness which gave each building its own expressive form. The decorative imagery reveals the style's romantic nature. Exotic birds, tropical flora, nymphs, sun rays, zigzags, and waves all make up the imagery in the bas-reliefs on the facades of these buildings. Birds used most often are the flamingo, heron and pelican, all native to the area. The depiction of human figures evolved from earlier languid Art Nouveau poses to a more sinewy, sultry and stylized pose. Naturalistic representation of nude figures was also frequent.

68

Since 1985 entrepreneurs, developers, owners and artists have transformed a square mile containing over 400 buildings in the Art Deco style. The area was designated as an Historic District by the National Register of Historic Places in 1979. Most recently they have all been repainted as modern white facades with panels of pastel colors and accents of neon lighting. The buildings are once again significant for the stylistic integrity of the design of each individual building and for the thematic harmony by which each one relates to the other and to the entire community of Miami Beach.

The Modern Movement had its roots in the Bauhaus, and was further developed by Walter Gropius, Le Corbusier and Mies van der Rohe, among others who established the International Style. Stark, smooth, flush surfaces, devoid of ornamentation except for the joining of materials, characterized this new style. As such, it was the death-blow to all architectural ornament. Yet, many American architects soon tired of the sterile and anemic facades.

69

After the blandness of the curtain-wall waned, modern architectural ornament was derived from the use of luxurious materials and the patterns created by their arrangement and method of joining. It became an architecture of joints, grids, and the stamped patterns of modular fabrications. The building itself became the ornament, yet its facade expressed nothing of the function within. It was sculptural, but on a flat plane. It was two-dimensional. The simplest way to ornament the facade was through the use of textured material, although generally repeated in exact uniformity throughout the entire facade.

ORNAMENT

The elements of ornamental detail include geometrical lines, natural foliage, artificial objects, animals and the human figure. These ingredients may be combined and applied in various arrangements or features according to certain principles or a certain period or style. The oldest forms of ornamentation consist of geometric figures, small circles, bands, and straight lines. Ornament arises from the desire to represent the objects of the external world. Nearest at hand are natural objects: plants, animals, and humans. Inorganic objects also offers models such as the crystalline forms of snowflakes and natural phenomena such as clouds, waves, and other patterns from nature. Artificial objects also offer a rich resource of forms, any of which may be combined with another. It is easy to combine details taken from nature into forms not found in nature to create the sphinx, centaur, mermaid, and other animal and human bodies with plantlike terminations.

Ornament is determined primarily by the design objective, the location on the facade, and the material, as well as the design ideas ruling at the period of the particular culture. The peculiarities that arise from the relationship of form and material are modified by the style of that particular period. Geometrical motifs are formed by the rhythmical arrangement of shapes, whereas natural motifs follow the vegetable, animal and human forms. Artificial objects are forms borrowed from art, technology or science, and usually take the form of symbols, trophies and the like. Ornament that relates to features of facades can be classified according to its function or application. These classifications include bands and borders, framing and connecting forms, free ornaments, supports, enclosed ornaments in panels, and repeated ornaments, as in friezes, cornices and corbel tables.

In nearly every style throughout history the plant world has been used in ornamental patterns. Each culture preferred the plant forms that were native to its own environment. The selection to incorporate plants was determined mostly by the beauty of the form and partly by its symbolic meaning. The use of animals in natural or idealized forms is considerable, but not as extensive as plant forms. The adaptation of animal forms to ornamentation was more difficult. The types of animals used for ornamental purposes were not the domestic ones, as one might expect, such as the horse and the dog. Rather, they were those that had a basis in historical symbolic reference, such as the griffin, eagle and lion.

The human form has always been a favored object of representation in art and ornament. There was a natural tendency to depict humans in nearly every culture and every design style. Even symbolic and supernatural powers were given a human form. The human body was also represented without any specific meaning or symbolism strictly on account of its beauty of form, such as applications of the human face more or less true to nature, as well as caricatures and masks, grotesques, and other strange combinations of human animal and plant elements. Partial human figures were also used as the starting point of ornament: half figures and those mixtures of half-human and half-animal that were characteristic of early sculpture, such as the sphinx and the centaur.

Besides geometrical elements and those copied from nature, there are a number of artificial objects, used either alone or in combination with the other two. Decorative groups of hunting and warlike implements and tools are trophies; the devices and representation of guilds and crafts are

symbols. It was the custom of the Greeks to hang the weapons that the enemy had left behind on the trunks of trees. These tokens of victory were also used by the Romans to adorn their monuments. They were used later in the architecture of castles, town halls, and tombs. The grouping of tools and instruments was expressed as symbols. Art, architecture, music, painting and sculpture, as well as science, astronomy, chemistry, commerce, handicrafts and trade were all expressed by symbols. The different trades have chosen their symbols partly from their tools, partly from their finished products. The guilds of past centuries introduced a graphic vocabulary into these visible signs of their trade.

Ornamental details started with joints. Mass-produced cast-iron and terra-cotta units were ordered through catalogs and bolted and assembled at the construction site. This was different from masonry construction with gravity load-bearing walls. Facade expanses with large openings and spacious interiors were now made possible. Terra-cotta became popular as an alternative to brownstone construction, because it was easy to produce and it stood up to changes in temperature. It was lighter than stone, so it could be used for higher buildings, and it was fireproof. In the 1870s the terra-cotta industry produced ornament for countless urban facades. Terra-cotta was used almost exclusively for ornamental details, as it could be carved and cast more easily than stone. It was glazed for use on nearly all Art Deco buildings. Terra-cotta was eventually replaced by steel in taller buildings.

Ornamental details determine the character and visual appearance of a building's facade. When ornamental details are removed from a facade, it looks looks barren and lifeless. The removed details that end up in museum gardens or sold by antique dealers look like empty shells that were removed from their husks.

The purpose of ornament is to embellish an object, but there are many variations to the process of ornamentation. In the first place, the use of ornament should always be intentional; and secondly, the ornament should always be integrally related to the building's structure and materials. The ornamentation can be limited to the the structural elements only, as in Gothic pinnacles, or Art Nouveau ironwork, or the diagonal bracing of the John Hancock Building in Chicago. The post and bracket of Carpenter Gothic houses is an example of a structurally related ornamental element. Fake structural elements have been used ornamentally, such as the mullions of certain curtainwall structures, the so-called "honest structures." Some ornament is simply applied and totally unrelated to the structure. Finally, the structure itself can be ornamental, such as those examples found in organic architecture.

The urge to embellish and the love of ornamental effect are basic to human nature. In all ages and all cultures the human race has demonstrated a persistent impulse to embellish its structures. By using ornament, people of every society have transformed the merely useful into the beautiful, giving meaning and importance to an often drab reality. Ornament is essentially a device to move the eye, to intrigue the mind, or simply to surprise and delight us.

Even though the essence of ornament is freedom from function, there are a number of practical necessities that ornament is able to satisfy. Ornament helps to identify elements on a facade. Moldings, lintels, cornices, and friezes help to distinguish the tops, middle portions and bases of buildings. Ornamental surrounds, for example, emphasize doors and windows in a facade. These ornamental details are devices which establish architectural scale and relate it to either a human or monumental scale. They break down the overall mass of a building into smaller parts that relate comfortably to the human observer. One reason we prefer older sections of cities to the newer urban environments is because their scale feels right to us. It is a focal point as well as a measuring point, whereby we can relate ourselves to a piece of architecture through its ornament and detail. This is particularly true when the detail contains human faces, figures, and those forms which are closest to our own being.

The monuments of antiquity and the buildings of early cultures shown in the opening chapter were designed during periods when ornament was not something that occurred after the structure was conceived. It was part of an integrated process. Architecture, painting, and sculpture were combined into one expression. We see the ruins of Greek temples as pristine white marble shrines, when in fact they were highly decorated with bright colors. There is similar evidence that Egyptian temples were also highly decorated, and some Egyptologists have claimed that the pyramids were covered with colorful designs. We see the Mayan temples as cold stone ruins, and we know they were carved profusely, but evidence shows that they were highly decorated in bright colors.

The Renaissance architect considered ornament and architecture as inseparable. Every element related to the whole. The wall was the ornament; the ornament was the wall. The same was true for columns, windows, doorways, and all the elements of the facade. Later styles began to develop ornament for its own sake as something other than structural, something other than functional. It was applied to the structure, technically useless, with the sole function of adding beauty. It took architects like Antonio Gaudi, Louis Sullivan, and other Art Nouveau designers to combine the two again.

Meanwhile, Austrian architect Adolf Loos and others were decrying that putting ornamental details on buildings was nothing short of a crime. The futurists published a manifesto declaring that ornament must be abolished. The Bauhaus nurtured these theories, which were carried out by the International Style proponents in Europe and America. Art Deco designers did not succumb totally to the dogma of the modernists, nor did Frank Lloyd Wright, who developed an integrated form of organic architecture, wherein ornament was once again related to the concept of the structure. Modernism is the first in the lineage of western styles that did not encourage or permit eclecticism. All former styles except Art Nouveau dipped into the pool of ornamental elements of the past. They incorporated those for which they had an affinity. The Modern Movement turned instead to the use of materials and refinement of detailing as its expression of ornament. The combination of materials and the juxtaposition of forms substituted for the use of ornament in the modern structure. Modern architects were limited to a vocabulary composed mainly of geometric structural elements, but it did not change the forms significantly since they came into fashion nearly half a century ago. A renewed interest in the use of architectural ornament will restore human interest and human scale to the structure, and give people a frame of reference by which they can relate to architecture once again.

AGRAFFE

The agraffe is an ornamental device which refers to the uppermost voissoir or keystone of an arch, especially when it is carved as a cartouche including a human face with ornamental embellishments. Originally, the top block locked the arch in place and was therefore the central piece. Rarely are the outside pieces of the curve of the arch ornamented, whereas continuous ornamentation around the inside of the arch often features decorative designs or figures.

There are unlimited variations on the design of a cartouche, and an equal number of varieties of the human face. When the two are combined the design possibilities are endless. The top to bottom center row of images are all from stone-faced structures in Paris. The top and bottom figures each have an unusual sideward glance, as opposed to the typical forward gaze. The small images in the center show a head and shoulders looking down as if shot from above, yet it was shot from the street below. The lower left figure, found in Philadelphia, gestures downward with her eyes apparently closed.

The top center panel shows a menacing face glaring from within ornamental scrolls. It was removed from its original location on a building and used as an ornamental window display. The images flanking it on each side illustrate how designs using naturalistic foliage are often interwoven with a human face. Often the face is simply suggested within the leafy design. These images appear in a large rusticated stone arch in downtown Portland. In the center panel, oak leaves are added to the face within the elaborate cartouche, which extends the design across the top of the arch.

Aegicranes are the sculptured representations of the heads and skulls of goats and rams, which were used as ornamentation on altars and friezes. Ram heads are a favorite form of corner or cornice ornament, and serve as objects from which to hang festoons. The decorative use in both cases is connected with the use of the ram as a sacrificial animal. At times the use of other fantastic assemblages are substituted, such as chimera heads or grotesques.

The skulls can be found on friezes, in panels, within medallions and in keystones of arches. The two top examples are part of a facade in New York City which is designed with a Mayan theme, and framed within the grid-like pilasters. The two skulls and female face in the left center are from a continuous frieze on a building in London. The long-horned skull within the elaborate cartouche on the bottom left panel appears on the Million Dollar Theater in Los Angeles. The skulls in the bottom low-relief panel flank a large window, with a mask and festoons above it and griffins below, on a New York City facade.

ANIMAL FORMS: BESTIARY

The bizarre images of beasts with leering faces and distorted bodies were once regarded as magical and intensely real. Belief in the power of mythical beasts to ward off evil spirits persisted throughout the Middle Ages. They were found on all types of ornament and facades of buildings. Animal imagery is an art as old as the caves of France. The fantastic creatures of the Romanesque and Gothic period were adapted from those used by the Greeks and Romans.

To create these animals, artists consulted a bestiary for real or imaginary examples that they would paint, carve, or cast. The bestiary was a collection of medieval allegorical fables about the habits and traits of animals; each fable was followed by an interpretation of its significance. Most church leaders encouraged the use of monsters as symbols of good and evil and used them in architecture and interior cloisters. By the Gothic period, artists and sculptors no longer took monsters seriously, and concentrated more on human forms or animal forms with human characteristics.

Many species of birds have been the subject of ornamentation throughout the ages. Many have been revered, such as the hawk in ancient Egypt. The owl is a nocturnal bird of prey with hooked and feathered talons, a large head with a short hooked beak and eyes set in a frontal plane. As such, the owl was a natural for selection as an ornamental design element. Images of the owl have appeared in many carvings, including ancient Greek coins.

Birds have been shown in ornamental detail in both a naturalistic fashion and grotesquely exaggerated forms. They often appear in medallions, as in the center image above, where the bird's tail becomes a serpent which ends up in the bird's mouth. The grotesque image of birds is popular on ornamental panels that flank entrances, as in the top left panel, or used in archivolts, as in the top right panel. In the center panel abstract metal birds are found above doorways. The large owl figures are on buildings at New York University. A mirror-image design in the capital is a device often used.

There are numerous examples of the cow, bull and bison used as motifs in ornamental sculpture and architectural ornament. Prime examples are the winged bull from Assyrian palaces, the carved cows and bulls on Egyptian temples, and the carved bulls on Indian architecture and sculpture. More recent examples are the heads of bison which appear on many midwestern and western facades. These motifs were used in capitals, corbels and bas-relief friezes.

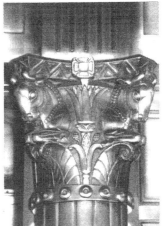

The center panel shows a bas-relief from the capitol building at Lincoln, where bison played an important role in western history. The abstract bull's head holds the cable to a metal canopy in New York. The carved bison head appears above a corbel on the travertine facade of a bank in Denver. The top right panel is a stylized head of a bull from an ornamental frieze framing a doorway in Kansas City. The steer head within the square frame appears on a converted slaughterhouse in New York's meat district. Twin bulls appear in place of the corner volutes in the capitals of an old New York City bank.

The family of canines includes dogs, wolves and foxes. Although the most popular of the group are dogs, their representation on buildings is rather limited. They are more often shown as derivatives or assemblages of other animals, such as chimeras. The top left image shows the face of a bulldog incised into a limestone facade above a doorway in New York City. The right one shows another bulldog that appears on a converted carriage house in New York city.

80

Chimeras are fantastic assemblages of animal forms so combined as to produce a single, complete but imaginary species. They are usually described as fire-breathing monsters and represented as a composite. Chimeras are found on panels and as gargoyles and capitals. The bottom center and right panel images are on the Parliament House in Toronto. The chimera in the stone panel inset into brick is on a residence in Chicago. The chimera capital at the bottom left is at the entrance to a New York building.

The eagle is the most representative of the feathered species. Size, strength, majestic flight and keen vision distinguish the eagle from other birds. The eagle has been used in ornamental details in Egypt, Assyria and Persia. The eagle was the companion of Zeus for the Greeks. The Romans chose the eagle for the standards of their legions. thus the frequent appearance of the eagle on emblems of war. The eagle appeared in heraldry at a very early period.

The eagle was incorporated into many designs in the United States as the national symbolic bird. In Seattle it was the symbol for the Fraternal Order of Eagles. The top left panel shows a modern adaptation of the bird executed in brass that guards a New York entrance. Most eagles are placed at strategic locations on pilasters, in capitals and in friezes, although it is often found as a standalone ornament. The designs are extremely varied, showing the eagle with upswept wings, outstretched wings, and in a downward folded position. In New York it is the symbol of a women's political organization.

82

Many materials are used in the depiction of eagles. They are carved from smooth limestone, textured granite, or veined marble. They were fashioned from metal, as in the top center panel. The eagle was fashioned into an entrance canopy in Rochester. The abstract metal eagle projecting from the wall of the Detroit Federal Building is a dramatic use of the birdlike form. The variety of forms fits the variety of uses for this decorative bird motif. The use of the double eagle provides even more variety, as seen in the column base in the bottom center panel of a government building in St. Louis.

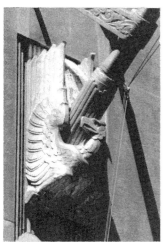

Next to the lion, the eagle is the creature used most often in ornamental work. The ornamental forms may vary considerably from the natural form. The eagle can be incised into stone, cut out of stone, or cast in metal. The large-scale sculpture in the top center panel stands guard outside a government building in New Orleans. The eagle is a favorite ornamental device to support flags on building facades. Some eagle forms are so geometric in design as to lose their identity, as seen in the lower right panel of an abstract eagle located on a post-office-building pylon in downtown Philadelphia.

The category of felines includes lions, tigers, jaguars, and domestic cats. Of these, the lion holds the first rank in ornamental fauna. Strength, courage and nobility have assured the lion the title of "king of beasts." The stature, compact build and striking muscles were all challenges to the sculptor. Lion hunts were common subjects on the palaces of Assyrian kings, and the distinctive rendering of muscles gave these idealized representations charm and grandeur.

84

The top center panel shows a crouching carved stone lion at the spring point of an arched doorway in Venice. To the left is one of the lions believed to be imported from Byzantium and installed in the Piazza San Marco under the well known bell chimes. The other lion is on the facade of St. Mark's. The image on the right is a giant lion head, over five feet tall, removed from a Renaissance building and displayed in a museum in Florence. Felines in every style and building material are found in nearly every city in the western world, since they were a popular ornamental motif on elements of a building's facade.

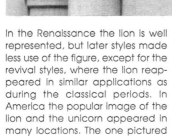

In the Renaissance the lion is well represented, but later styles made less use of the figure, except for the revival styles, where the lion reappeared in similar applications as during the classical periods. In America the popular image of the lion and the unicorn appeared in many locations. The one pictured with the clock is over an entryway in Boston. Whether the lion was represented in a naturalistic state or stylized, it was used at every opportunity in capitals, as pilaster ornaments, in medallions, keystones of arches and windows, and in bas-relief sculptures throughout the country.

The lion head has been more extensively applied to building facades than the entire body. It is found as a gargoyle, on corbels, as keystones, on door knockers, and as a purely decorative element on pilasters and capitals. Panther and tiger heads are sometimes found in antiquity, and are used in similar applications. In all styles the representation of the eyes of the lion are much closer to the oval eye of humans than to the round eye of the feline species.

The row of lion's heads in the top center panel punctuates the cornice of an ornate window in New Orleans. The lion head popping out of the top of a shield is a corner ornament at the base of a column in Nashville. Lion's heads appear in many other ornamental features on the facade, such as in keystones, under corbels, in pilaster capitals, and within cartouches. There is perhaps no other animal form that ever achieved such a widespread ornamental use.

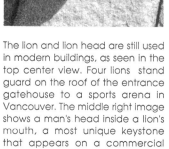

The lion and lion head are still used in modern buildings, as seen in the top center view. Four lions stand guard on the roof of the entrance gatehouse to a sports arena in Vancouver. The middle right image shows a man's head inside a lion's mouth, a most unique keystone that appears on a commercial building in New York City. On the bottom left, the square panel with the head of a feline set inside it appears above the door on a stone facade in Washington, D.C. The terra-cotta lion head in the bottom right and center panels appears under a corbel on a brick wall in New Orleans.

In addition to imitations of natural animals, there have been various monsters composed of parts of several different animals. Centaurs and sphinxes are examples. The combination of different animals produces forms that are consid- ered grotesque or fantastic. The chief representative of this form is the griffin, which is the union of a lion's body with the head and wings of an eagle. The fore section may be that of either the lion or the eagle.

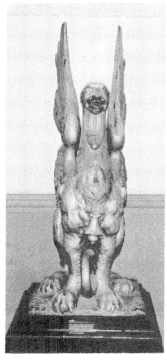

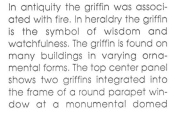

In antiquity the griffin was associated with fire. In heraldry the griffin is the symbol of wisdom and watchfulness. The griffin is found on many buildings in varying ornamental forms. The top center panel shows two griffins integrated into the frame of a round parapet window at a monumental domed structure in Paris. Below it are two griffins of Assyrian influence standing guard over the doorway on a New York City apartment. The flanking griffins in the top panels were removed from their location on a power utilities building in Rochester and installed as sculptures in the renovated lobby.

Grotesques are sculptured ornaments involving fanciful distortions of animal forms that are sometimes combined with plant motifs. These may contain a variety of forms which have no counterpart in nature. They project from the upper section of roofs in Gothic architecture, and are designed to carry small quantities of rainwater from the upper spires and towers. The rainwater drips over the nose of the beast and not through its mouth, as in the case of gargoyles.

Common characteristics are found in grotesques such as the use of wings or a tail of floral ornamentation at the end of the form. The top left creature makes up the bracket for a flagpole projecting from a New York City building. In the center, a salamander hovers over the doorway to a landmark restaurant in New York. In Chicago, the helmeted birdlike creature looms over each side of an entryway. A tentacled serpent holds up a balcony in New York City, and lionlike forms with wings and tails embellish doorways and spandrel panels. Intertwined double-winged birds are seen on a capital in New York.

The horse rarely appears as an isolated figure. The legs are too thin to be rendered in anything but metal. This limitation does not affect the use of the horse in bas-relief, where it is often found. Horses often appear in groups of two or three, and nearly always shown in overlapping profiles. The horse is mostly shown along with a rider, or a figure leading the horse. They are found atop pediments as in the top center image of roof statuary on a building in Philadelphia.

Horse heads on medallions signify stables and carriage houses, and the top right example appears in New York City. The top left horse and rider remains in its niche since Renaissance times on a Milan facade. A widely used variation of the horse is the centaur, an imaginary creature with the forepart of a man and the hindpart of a horse. The centaur frieze appears over the entrance to a university building in Cincinnati. The bas-relief of horse and rider at the bottom is from a cement plaster facade in Munich. The metal gilded horse and rider are part of an ornamental door frame in Cincinnati.

Among the many sources for ornamental designs are creatures of the sea. Among them the dolphin has been the most widely used. These sea mammals have always enjoyed a veneration which protects them from potential harm.

They appear on antique coins and on Graeco-Italic terra-cotta, on Pompeian mural paintings, and as ornamentation on many Greek and Roman facades. The dolphin motif is often used in pilasters, panels, ceilings and fountains.

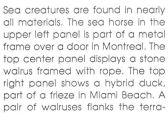

Sea creatures are found in nearly all materials. The sea horse in the upper left panel is part of a metal frame over a door in Montreal. The top center panel displays a stone walrus framed with rope. The top right panel shows a hybrid duck, part of a frieze in Miami Beach. A pair of walruses flanks the terra-cotta corner pilaster in Seattle. The center panel shows a parapet detail from the Marine Building in Vancouver, which features the trident and other sea creatures. The two bottom images show scenes from a bronze frieze wrapping around the lower story of a New York city office building.

91

There are animals of every description that adorn and embellish buildings throughout the world. Each country and culture has its own native species. In India the elephant is used frequently. In America it is rarely seen. America is the melting pot not only of humans but animals from all over the globe. Many were found here in the wild; others were imported. There is an organization in New York City whose sole purpose is to foster appreciation for animals on buildings.

The top center panel displays how animals and humans are blended to form ornamental details over doorways and as corbels. The top flanking panels feature gargoyle-like cement creatures at the parapet level of a brick structure. The left figure is a rhinoceros and the right one an elephant. Smaller animals such as squirrels have their place in panels, plaques, and as label stops at windows. The rabbit and lamb at the lower left is part of a capital on one of New York's most animal-laden entrance to an apartment house. The double-image salamander is above the entrance to a Vancouver building.

Ram heads are a favorite form of ornamental motif for keystones and cornices, and serve as objects from which to hang festoons. The ram's head represents wisdom, power, strength and a defender of right. It was a popular motif from a design standpoint as well, due to the ornamental characteristics associated with the curving horns. It was mostly used in a frontal view, and only occasionally in profile. The ram's head can be found on many parts of building facades

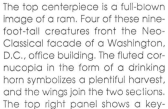

The top centerpiece is a full-blown image of a ram. Four of these nine-foot-tall creatures front the Neo-Classical facade of a Washington, D.C., office building. The fluted cornucopia in the form of a drinking horn symbolizes a plentiful harvest, and the wings join the two sections. The top right panel shows a keystone of a free-standing pavillion in Portland. The center image shows the ram in profile on a pilaster capital in New York City. A ram's head in Des Moines hold cables to support a metal canopy. The ram's head keystone appears at the entrance to the American Woolen Building in New York City.

ANIMAL FORMS: SPHINX

The sphinx is a combination of the body of one animal with the head of another. It appeared first in Egypt, as the great sphinx of Memphis. The Greek version was a mythological female monster represented by the body of a lion with the head and breasts of a woman. She was said to have posed riddles to those who passed by, and killed all who couldn't guess the answer. The sphinx was the guardian of temples and tombs, and often believed to be symbolic of wisdom.

The sphinx still holds a fascination for designers and the public. In Las Vegas, sphinxes are found in several locations along the casino strip. At Caesar's Palace there is a pavillion with a sphinx guardian. In another location there is a pair of bronze sphinxes flanking the entry. The bottom row of images shows a bronze sculpture originally designed for an exposition in Toronto. The sphinxes follow the Egyptian precedent in the use of the male head and headdress, with the upper body of a woman and the lower body of a lion. The sphinxes support a large globe upon which stands a symbolic winged statue.

ANIMAL FORMS: WINGED

There are many figures with wings among the ornamental motifs found on facades. These include birds, eagles, angels, grotesques, cherubs, and the caduceus of Mercury among them. The use of winged figures appears as early as the Tower of the Winds in Greece, and was a device used throughout the Renaissance to fill the spandrel of an arch. Wings were useful devices to complete a figure, or to give grotesques a menacing character if desired.

The wings were applied to griffins, grotesques, and other monsters. The top center panel shows a griffin-like sculptural creature used in a memorial fountain in front of a classical facade. The top right panel shows a winged creature as a corner finial in a stucco parapet ornamented with faces and dolphins, located in Santa Monica. The bottom center panel shows a winged bull inspired by Assyrian motifs, above the doorway of a New York City apartment building. The winged carved stone creature in the bottom left panel is located on a high parapet on Toronto's Parliament House.

Arcades are derived from covered walkways supported by pillars and a line of arches either freestanding or attached to a building. Some enclose shops along one or both sides. More specifically an arcade refers to any covered space lit from the top and lined with shops on one or more levels. The arcade style was perfected until it became quite sophisticated in design, with ornamental exteriors and interior facades. Ornamental figures were used on the exterior and interior.

The top row shows the Royal Arcade in London, where sculpture and bas-relief ornamentation embellish both the exterior and interior facades. Half-figure caryatids flank each corner of the pediment, and bas-relief panels flank each side. The bottom row shows one of the earliest arcades, built in Brussels in the Neo-Classical style. It features sculptural panels on the exterior facade, with a repeat of the motifs on the interior arcade facades. The central area was covered by a long iron and glass skylight which extended in a cross pattern to connect several streets. It is located near the Grand Place.

The architrave is the lowest of the three divisions of an entablature. It is the main beam that spans from column to column and rests directly on the capitals. This part of the entablature has always been ornamented, often with faces, figures, or geometric designs. The top center panel shows the macabre image of alternating skulls and faces of cherubs. An example in Florence shows a conglomeration of ornamentation in a medieval-style entryway.

An archivolt is the ornamental molding running around the exterior curved surface of an arch or around the openings of doors and windows. The designs can be geometric or naturalistic, and can include figures. Some archivolts recede in a stepped fashion, which results in stepped pilasters, often ornamented with fantastic assemblages of faces, figures and animal forms. The bottom center panel shows such a design on the entry to a bank in Vancouver.

A balcony is a projecting platform, generally on the exterior facade of a building. It is sometimes supported from below, sometimes cantilevered, enclosed with a railing, balustrade or other vertical parapet. It can be supported from below by brackets or corbels, projecting members of wood, metal, or masonry. Balconies are designed as an integral part of the structure, and are plain or ornamental depending entirely on the style of the building facade.

The top row of images shows details of a balcony on an apartment house in Paris. It is supported by three armless caryatids. The metal balcony railing has a lacy design that does not obscure the figures. The central row of images show a balcony in Augsburg in which male figures are posed to support the weight of the balcony. They are cast of the same material as the facade. The bottom row of images displays a pair of caryatids above an entry to a Paris restaurant, holding the balcony above with an outstretched arm, apparently with little effort. They are similat to figures on the Opera House in Paris.

The form of balconies is a design concern and a structural problem, as balconies may be supported on brackets or corbels. The top left panel shows the balcony of the Furstenburg Palace in Innsbruck. In Chicago, a false balcony is supported by corbels incorporating small grotesque masks. The solid parapet is carved with grotesques. On the top right a Parisian apartment house combines sculpture and ornamental iron to provide a focal point on the facade. In the center panel a figure leers from the soffit of a baroque bacony in Paris, and four faces highlight the soffit of an Art Nouveau balcony in Paris.

Bands are all the ornamental forms that border, frame, or connect parts of the facade elements. The motifs used can be geometrical, naturalistic or a combination. The band has no limitation on length, but is generally a narrow ribbon-like ornament. The principal ornaments used in bands are the fret, chain and interlacing bands. The Greek fret is one of the more popular motifs and is of textile design origin. The forerunners are from Egyptian and Assyrian styles.

Bands oftentimes are highlighted or punctuated with heads of lions or human faces. In the top center panel a female face peers out from a naturalistic band of carved stone on a Romanesque Revival church in Newark. In Philadelphia the glazed terra-cotta band of geometric ornament hangs like a festoon between the hexagonal openings on an office building. The interlaced band consists of varied forms passing over and under one another, and woven together to run continuously for any length in a horizontal direction. They are used as borders and run around arches and door openings.

BRACKET

A bracket is a projection from a vertical surface which provides structural or visual support under cornices, balconies, window frames or any other overhanging member. Brackets vary in form depending on the material and location on the facade. Usually they are used to support cornices or door and window lintels. When small, plain brackets are used to support a cornice, they are called modillions. Brackets were popular elements to feature carved faces and figures.

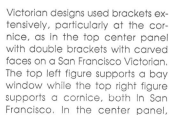

Victorian designs used brackets extensively, particularly at the cornice, as in the top center panel with double brackets with carved faces on a San Francisco Victorian. The top left figure supports a bay window while the top right figure supports a cornice, both in San Francisco. In the center panel, brackets support a Venetian balcony. The large carved wooden head in the bottom panel supports an entry canopy in Heidelburg, and the baby face is part of a side door in the Milan Cathedral. Renaissance buildings show the use of brackets to support upper floors in the lower right example in Florence.

BRIDGES

There are many famous bridges throughout the world. One of those is the Bridge of Sighs in Venice, connecting the Doge's Palace, where the tribunal courts were held, with the prison across a narrow canal. From the inside it was the last view of freedom afforded prisoners as they passed over the bridge to incarceration. From the outside, it is a romantic feature, with its elliptical arch, rusticated pilasters, heraldic devices, and row of human faces across the bottom of the arch.

Another bridge made famous by the venetian painter Canelletto is the Rialto Bridge over the Grand Canal in Venice. The base of the bridge at each side of the canal contains a bas-relief sculpture that features a marine scene. The bridge includes a series of covered shops that line the inclined passageway. At the apex a pitched roof structure features a large human face. Other bridges in Venice repeat the marine theme in bas-relief sculptures at the base. Since Venice has perhaps more bridges than any other city in the world, the marine theme is very commonplace.

BRIDGES

The Ponte Vecchio in Florence is the oldest bridge in the city, with its segmental arches springing from massive piers, built to withstand the floods. The small shops of the goldsmith's quarters line both sides of the roadway. The bridge has an architectural character that relates to the Renaissance buildings on both sides of the bridge. The corridor above the roadway was added by the architect Vasari to allow passage by the clergy from the Uffizzi palace to the church.

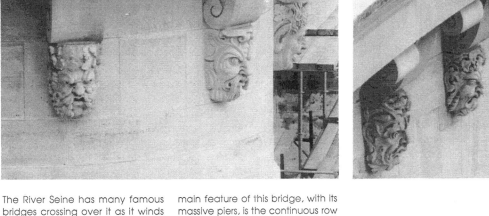
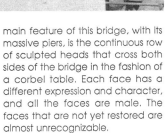

The River Seine has many famous bridges crossing over it as it winds through Paris. One of those is the Pont Neuf, which is undergoing extensive restoration and cleaning. (It is discouraging how the "City of Light" has become so dark, as grime accumulated on its monuments, buildings and bridges.) The main feature of this bridge, with its massive piers, is the continuous row of sculpted heads that cross both sides of the bridge in the fashion of a corbel table. Each face has a different expression and character, and all the faces are male. The faces that are not yet restored are almost unrecognizable.

The capital is the upper member of a column, pillar, pier or pilaster. It is usually decorated, and may carry an architrave, arcade or impost block. In classical architecture each of the Orders had its own respective capital, which differed significantly from one another. In later periods capitals became endlessly diversified. The bifront capital is one which has two faces, looking in two directions, the quadrifront capital has four faces, looking in four directions.

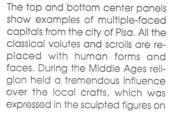

The top and bottom center panels show examples of multiple-faced capitals from the city of Pisa. All the classical volutes and scrolls are replaced with human forms and faces. During the Middle Ages religion held a tremendous influence over the local crafts, which was expressed in the sculpted figures on capitals more than anywhere else. They were closer to eye level than the distant gargoyles on the upper levels. The capitals symbolically illustrated common events, with crude imagery combining human figures, animal shapes, natural vegatation and building elements into fantastic and grotesque forms.

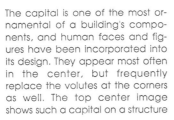

The capital is one of the most ornamental of a building's components, and human faces and figures have been incorporated into its design. They appear most often in the center, but frequently replace the volutes at the corners as well. The top center image shows such a capital on a structure in Venice, where a female figure replaces all four volutes of a Corinthian capital. The lower right image shows a similar treatment, where four winged felines replace the volutes and frame a center cherub. The lower left image features a corner capital above which is a circular frieze of faces.

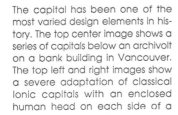

The capital has been one of the most varied design elements in history. The top center image shows a series of capitals below an archivolt on a bank building in Vancouver. The top left and right images show a severe adaptation of classical Ionic capitals with an enclosed human head on each side of a door in Milan. The two left panels below it show rare examples of capitals with Egyptian motifs. The middle image is from a religious building in San Francisco, and the lower one from an eclectic exterior in New York City. The bottom right image shows an adaptation of the same motif in a cast-iron capital.

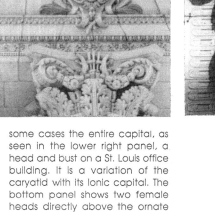

Since the predominant style of building in America has been adaptations of classical forms in various revival styles, the design of capitals was varied. Yet the use of the human head as an ornamental device never disappeared altogether. It often replaced the center portion of the capital, or in some cases the entire capital, as seen in the lower right panel, a head and bust on a St. Louis office building. It is a variation of the caryatid with its Ionic capital. The bottom panel shows two female heads directly above the ornate capitals in the architrave of a New York City theater.

107

A cartouche is an elaborate decorative ornamental tablet resembling a scroll of paper with the center either inscribed or left plain. It is framed with an elaborate scroll-like carving. Cartouches are often accompanied by human figures, either cherubs or young females. The cartouche is found on many different parts of a facade, but most often at the parapet, over openings of doors and windows. The design variations on the cartouche are endless.

Early forms of the cartouche are inspired more by symbolism than ornamental concerns. The upper left image from Venice features a shrouded skull; the upper right image from Florence shows a lion inside a medallion. The central image is a cartouche on a corner in Augsburg. The female half-figure to the left ends in a flowing design; the right figure is a grotesque male. The lower left image features two cherubs flanking an elaborate cartouche in the entrance soffit of a New York theater. The lower right image is on a blank wall in New York City, and features male sculptures and a mask symbol below.

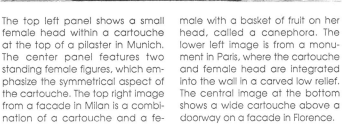

The top left panel shows a small female head within a cartouche at the top of a pilaster in Munich. The center panel features two standing female figures, which emphasize the symmetrical aspect of the cartouche. The top right image from a facade in Milan is a combination of a cartouche and a female with a basket of fruit on her head, called a canephora. The lower left image is from a monument in Paris, where the cartouche and female head are integrated into the wall in a carved low relief. The central image at the bottom shows a wide cartouche above a doorway on a facade in Florence.

The clock and its predecessor, the sundial, have been used as ornamental devices since ancient times. From the medieval period until the early 1800s the sundial appeared on many structures. It was usually surrounded by the signs of the zodiac, and was often executed in mosaic tile with gilded zodiac figures. Clocks have been built into various parts of building facades, often including ornamental details, animals and figures as part of the design.

The center image is the entrance to a bank in Oakland, and the elaborate clock has flanking male and female figures carved into the design. The top left image shows a clock incorporated into a facade in Munich. The top right clock encompasses the entire wall of a facade spaning a roadway in Brussels. The left images show two intricate clocks on facades in Innsbruck. The top one includes signs of the zodiac within the dial; the lower one appears on a tower flanked by metal gargoyles. The bottom center image is a mechanical clock with figurines pulling bell chimes on a facade in London.

A corbel is a projecting stone or piece of timber which supports another piece above it. In masonry, it is the sequential stepping out of bricks or stones to form an outward projection as it rises. In masonry construction small projecting parts need support from below; the corbel is such a device. Thus, this ornament was born from the practical requirements of specific construction materials and techniques. Corbel tables are continuous rows supporting cornices or parapets.

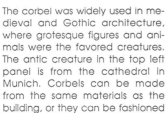

The corbel was widely used in medieval and Gothic architecture, where grotesque figures and animals were the favored creatures. The antic creature in the top left panel is from the cathedral in Munich. Corbels can be made from the same materials as the building, or they can be fashioned from a contrasting material such as terra-cotta or cast stone. Human figures and faces play an important role in the design of corbels. The two center panels show corbels that support cornices in New York City. The bottom center left image is a crouched figure supporting a bay window in Montreal.

111

112

The top center panel shows a corbel table on an apartment house in New York City. The rough, dark brick is contrasted by the smooth glazed terra-cotta corbels. The figures include rams, elephants, and grotesque masks. At the top left, a male head supports a column on an arched doorway in New York City. In the center, a bearded male and a female with matching flowing hair appear on the facade of a building in Paris. Across the bottom row are large female figures sculpted in clay, and cast as terra-cotta corbel ornaments supporting a long cornice on a New York City office structure.

CORNICE

A cornice is the upper projecting part of an entablature in classical architecture. It is supported by ornamental brackets or consoles. The cornice usually features a band of ornament running horizontally across its face. This band may be punctuated with ornamental devices: lions heads, animal heads, or human faces. A cornice can occur below the uppermost roof or parapet line. These lower cornices divide the wall surface at floor levels or over openings.

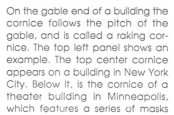

On the gable end of a building the cornice follows the pitch of the gable, and is called a raking cornice. The top left panel shows an example. The top center cornice appears on a building in New York City. Below it, is the cornice of a theater building in Minneapolis, which features a series of masks along the top. The top left panel shows a closeup of the capital and face above it. The center panels show cornices with bands of human heads. The bottom row shows ornate cornices from period buildings in San Francisco. The center image is the cornice of a cast-iron structure in New York City.

Doors are hinged, sliding, tilting or folding panels for closing openings in a wall or at entrances on the facades of buildings. From the times of the Romans doors were made of wood, metal and occasionally of marble. They turned on pivots working in slots. Later, hinges were used, which became ornamented, as were the handles. In the fourteenth century panels were introduced and became the main form of ornamentation, as they became more elaborately worked.

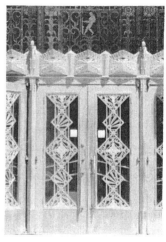

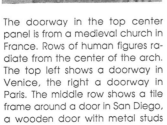

The doorway in the top center panel is from a medieval church in France. Rows of human figures radiate from the center of the arch. The top left shows a doorway in Venice, the right a doorway in Paris. The middle row shows a tile frame around a door in San Diego, a wooden door with metal studs and carved figures in Florence, a metal door in Heidelberg, and a metal door in New York City. The bottom row shows an Art Nouveau-inspired door in Montreal, an artist's loft door in New York City, an anamorphic design in Los Angeles, and a delicate wooden door frame with etched glass in Paris.

DOORKNOCKER

Although there are examples of the door knocker in ancient Greece, the period of highest use was in the Romanesque, Gothic and Renaissance periods. In modern times it has been replaced by the doorbell and bell chime. The door knocker was made almost exclusively of cast bronze. Its dimensions were variable, being related to the scale of the doorway, yet it had to relate to the human hand that operated it as well. These examples are from Renaissance buildings in Florence.

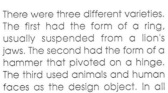

There were three different varieties. The first had the form of a ring, usually suspended from a lion's jaws. The second had the form of a hammer that pivoted on a hinge. The third used animals and human faces as the design object. In all three cases the noise is produced by the moveable part falling onto a metal stud. In the third example, the plate affixed to the door is of secondary importance, as the emphasis is focused on the countenance of the subject.

115

The doorway is the key area of interest in a facade, not only because it is the main focal point, but it offers an object to relate to a human scale. The framework that surrounds the door either has ornamented moldings around it or namented moldings around it or additional moldings over the top, which are supported by a large console at each end. While an overhead projection may shelter a doorway from rain, other forms of ornamentation further emphasize the visual appeal of the entrance.

The top row shows an intricately detailed Spanish Baroque entryway to a San Francisco apartment building. The repetitive designs were cast in stone. In the middle row the use of metal for the design of the doorway makes the intricate geometric design possible. The right images show the entrance to a New York City restaurant, where two terra-cotta cherubs form a corbel on the facade. The doorway shown on the bottom row is at the corner of a building in New Orleans. The large winged figure holding a pair of giant cornucopia complements the baroque nature of the entryway.

The doorway to the Brown Palace Hotel in Denver features images from nature that surround a young female face. The doorway in the middle left panel, in Rothenburg, has flanking male and female faces at the base of the columns, and male and female grotesques below the tympanum. The two right images show a doorway in Philadelphia featuring a terra-cotta young male between the two large circular windows above each door. The bottom row shows the cement plaster forms of young boys which appear over an entrance to a New York City apartment building.

The word "facade" comes from the Latin *facies*, face, and has come to mean the main face or elevation of a building as seen from the street or other public place. The elements that are brought together can be any type and be divided into groups relating to the wall surface, structure, fenestration and ornamentation. It is still the most essential architectural element and the most capable of communicating the function and significance of a building.

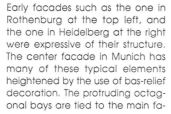

Early facades such as the one in Rothenburg at the top left, and the one in Heidelberg at the right were expressive of their structure. The center facade in Munich has many of these typical elements heightened by the use of bas-relief decoration. The protruding octagonal bays are tied to the main facade with bands of ornament in a frieze that connects them across the facade. Every part of the facade is sculpted in low-relief stucco, featuring festoons, cartouches, medallions, plaques and panels, all displaying sculptural faces, figures, and ornamental detail of every possible description.

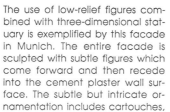

The use of low-relief figures combined with three-dimensional statuary is exemplified by this facade in Munich. The entire facade is sculpted with subtle figures which come forward and then recede into the cement plaster wall surface. The subtle but intricate ornamentation includes cartouches, festoons, cherubs, satyrs, and many other human faces and figures. Flanking each side of the entrance is a pair of figures which spring out of the pillars to become full statuary, on one side a young male figure, on the other a young female holding a torch. The figures are all human scale.

119

FESTOON / FIGURES: ADAM AND EVE

Fruit, tied in a bunch with leaves and flowers, was a popular motif of the Romans. The clusters hanging in curves are called festoons, and they decorated pilasters and panels. They sometimes hang between rosettes or skulls of animals.

The empty space above the curve was often filled with rosettes, masks, and figures. One variation on the festoon was the cornucopia, or classical "horn of plenty". The horn of a goat was used in ancient Greece to hold liquids and fruits.

A popular theme for religious figures in bas-relief and sculptures on religious structures was Adam and Eve. They were always accompanied by the serpent, a tree, and the apple. This motif was usually located near entryways or other conspicuous locations. The bottom left image is from Notre Dame in Paris. The middle horizontal carving of Eve is from a fourteenth-century French church. The bottom left center image is from a medieval French church, while the bottom right center figures are from a church in Rothenburg. The bottom right couple appears on the corner of a building in Venice.

FIGURES: ATLANTES

A Greek myth related that Atlas, one of the family of giant Titans, was defeated by Zeus after a long battle. The Titans were severely punished, especially Atlas, who was forced to hold up the heavens with his arms for eternity. The term "atlantes" describes these male figures used in place of columns as supports. As a natural counterpart to the caryatid, which is often found at the upper levels of a structure, the atlantes are usually found on the ground level.

The figures in the top center panel are at the main entrance to the Linderhoff Castle, where they support the entire facade. The right top image shows a male half-figure on a pilaster in Augsburg. The top left doorway in Rothenburg is flanked by two full-length figures. The images below are integrated into the entry piers. The center panel shows half-figures under a balcony in Brussels, along with the two figures seated on a pilaster. The small child holding up a bracket in the middle right panel is located in Venice. The three young male figures at the bottom support a small domed roof in Florence.

121

The term "bas-relief" refers to sculptural decoration in low relief in which none of the figures or motifs are separated from their backgrounds and project less than half their true proportions from the wall or surface. When the projection is equal to half the true proportion, it is called mezzo-relievo. When the projection is more than half, it is called alto-relievo. Double-aspect sculpture is halfway between relief and sculpture in the round to be viewed from all sides.

The word zodiac comes from the Greek zoidiakos, meaning "circle of carved figures". The carved bas-relief figures that surround the door frame of a New York City office building features all of the twelve astrological signs bearing the names of the constellations. Across the top of the door is a bas-relief frieze of figures. On the sides each sign is carved within the same double-arched frame. The middle row shows the figures for May (Pisces), August (Leo), September (Virgo), and October (Libra). On the bottom row two groups of figures are carved into a limestone wall on a plaza in Brussels.

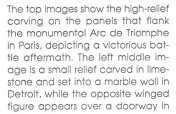

The top images show the high-relief carving on the panels that flank the monumental Arc de Triomphe in Paris, depicting a victorious battle aftermath. The left middle image is a small relief carved in limestone and set into a marble wall in Detroit, while the opposite winged figure appears over a doorway in the same city. The bottom row depicts a large relief whose edges are incised into the limestone facade. The large central figure of Columbia holds a torch and shaft of wheat. The panel appears at Rockefeller Center in New York City, and depicts a theme of family life, agriculture, and culture.

123

124

The top panel depicts a relief carving of Ceres, goddess of the harvest, joined by a cherub holding shafts of grain. Flanking left and right panels show a similar theme of industry and agriculture on the entrance panels to a government building in New Orleans. The small center panel shows a winged figure incised into the parapet on a Detroit government building. The bottom relief shows a draped figure of Columbia, symbol of the United States, filling a tall panel on a Kansas City government building. The bottom center panel shows a stucco relief of two figures within an ornamental frieze in Hollywood.

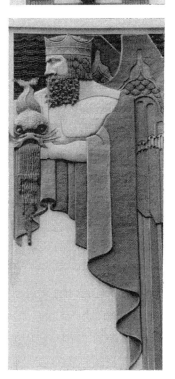
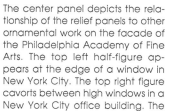

The center panel depicts the relationship of the relief panels to other ornamental work on the facade of the Philadelphia Academy of Fine Arts. The top left half-figure appears at the edge of a window in New York City. The top right figure cavorts between high windows in a New York City office building. The lower row of images are giant relief panels that were recently restored and re-painted with a modern palette. They are located near Grand Central Station in New York City, and are positioned over the building's two entrances. The distinctive style is Art Deco combined with a slight Assyrian influence.

carved or molded in the form of a draped female figure, either in high relief or sculpture in the round. According to legend, caryatids are imitations of virgins who danced at the temple in Carya at the feast of the Goddess Diana.

One of the most decorative motifs for supports is the use of human figures, and they have been used extensively since ancient times. The term "caryatid" refers to any supporting member serving the function of a pier or column that is

126

The caryatid in the top left panel appears between two large windows on a facade in Augsburg. The top center panel shows a sculpted figure in place of columns on a facade in Brussels. The right top caryatid appears at the corner of a Neo-Classical building in New York City. The caryatid carries the Ionic capital on her head. The bottom row shows the use of caryatids at doorways; the left and right panels show pairs of figures flanking doorways in Paris. The bottom center image shows the use of metallic figures in an Art Nouveau-inspired commercial doorway in London.

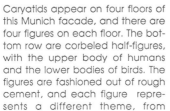

Caryatids appear on four floors of this Munich facade, and there are four figures on each floor. The bottom row are corbeled half-figures, with the upper body of humans and the lower bodies of birds. The figures are fashioned out of rough cement, and each figure represents a different theme, from motherhood to old age. The use of caryatids was carried forward in nearly all revival styles. In Brussels, two pairs of double caryatids support a pediment. The Philadelphia City Hall has numerous faces, figures and caryatid and atlantes figures supporting pediments on every corner of the structure.

According to the Roman architect Vitruvius, their use stems from the capture of women at Carya, who were held as prisoners and forced to carry heavy weights on their heads as punishment. The Middle Ages made little use of caryatids, whereas they were used extensively during the Renaissance. They occur on facades both as isolated figures and connected with the walls. The most well-known example is on the Porch of the Maidens of the Erechtheum at the Acropolis.

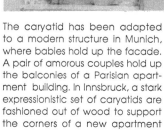 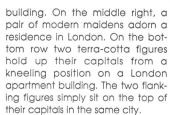

The caryatid has been adapted to a modern structure in Munich, where babies hold up the facade. A pair of amorous couples hold up the balconies of a Parisian apartment building. In Innsbruck, a stark expressionistic set of caryatids are fashioned out of wood to support the corners of a new apartment building. On the middle right, a pair of modern maidens adorn a residence in London. On the bottom row two terra-cotta figures hold up their capitals from a kneeling position on a London apartment building. The two flanking figures simply sit on the top of their capitals in the same city.

In the Renaissance and later derivations of the style, cherubs were used in decorative sculpture, on friezes, and on other parts of facades. They are represented as chubby, usually naked infants. They are also called putti and amorini. They are sometimes shown with wings. Their small size made them very adaptable to various parts of building ornamentation. They fit neatly into spandrels, friezes, and as accessories around door and window lintels.

The frieze at the top places four standing cherubs on each side of a central wreath. It appears over an entrance to a university fine-arts building in Cincinnati. On the left middle panel a cherub stands on top of a window ledge in Paris, and below, a pair of cherubs flank a cartouche. On the right middle panel, a group of cherubs explore the scientific world with beakers and thermometer, and the cherubs in the center panel cavort with a dolphin. The cherub in the lower right plays a horn on a New York brownstone spandrel, and the bottom panel shows one riding on a grotesque monster.

129

Many structures recognize the eminent people for whom they were built, or other historic personages in the design of the facade. This recognition can take the form of a plaque with the name of the individual inscribed within it, or a medallion with a portrait, or a bust with a sculpted figure. The bust represents the upper part of the human figure including the head, neck, and shoulders. It is usually set into a niche with a concave background.

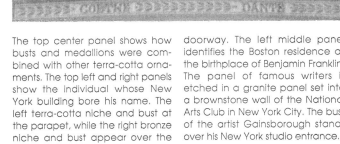

The top center panel shows how busts and medallions were combined with other terra-cotta ornaments. The top left and right panels show the individual whose New York building bore his name. The left terra-cotta niche and bust at the parapet, while the right bronze niche and bust appear over the doorway. The left middle panel identifies the Boston residence as the birthplace of Benjamin Franklin. The panel of famous writers is etched in a granite panel set into a brownstone wall of the National Arts Club in New York City. The bust of the artist Gainsborough stands over his New York studio entrance.

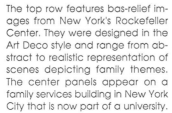

The top row features bas-relief images from New York's Rockefeller Center. They were designed in the Art Deco style and range from abstract to realistic representation of scenes depicting family themes. The center panels appear on a family services building in New York City that is now part of a university. The family theme is quite strong. The bottom left and right image appear in Augsburg on an otherwise plain stucco facade. The male and female figures are separated by a large expanse. The bottom center panel shows a medieval-style mother and child on a Brooklyn apartment building.

131

The family unit in earlier periods was usually represented only by mother and child. In later periods the family unit became a stronger theme for bas-relief sculptures. In Lincoln, Nebraska the unassuming long facade of an insurance company's headquarters is punctuated with a single framed bas-relief panel featuring a family unit. The group is encompassed within a large hand which forms the background of the high relief. The message is immediate and obvious.

WOODMEN ACCIDENT AND LIFE COMPANY

132

The Santa Monica Place shopping mall is adjacent to the Pacific Ocean. Across from the mall is a large monolithic structure broken only by horizontal bands of reveals. It is the Sear's department store. On the long facade are two large bas-reliefs featuring family units, which face each other. The unit is split into mother and child and father and child in the second panel. The wavy lines at the bottom of the figures relate to the oceanfront setting of the building.

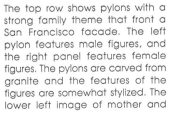

The top row shows pylons with a strong family theme that front a San Francisco facade. The left pylon features male figures, and the right panel features female figures. The pylons are carved from granite and the features of the figures are somewhat stylized. The lower left image of mother and children appears on a Munich facade along with fifteen other caryatids. On the opposite lower panel a half-figure of a mother and two children appears on a pilaster in Rothenburg. In the bottom center panels are two seated females doing household chores. They appear on a wall in Brussels.

The word grotesque is derived from "grotto," and refers to the fantastic, often ugly creatures produced by the fanciful distortion and combination of human, animal, and plant organisms in the freest and most arbitrary manner. Squatting, winged female figures without arms and human bodies with fishtails and endlessly long necks and with extremities ending in foliage are examples of this type of ornamentation. Pompeian art offers many clues as to their origin.

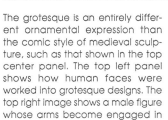

134

The grotesque is an entirely different ornamental expression than the comic style of medieval sculpture, such as that shown in the top center panel. The top left panel shows how human faces were worked into grotesque designs. The top right image shows a male figure whose arms become engaged in the volutes of a capital in Rothenburg. The bottom figures are corbels from the Chicago Tribune Tower building. The inspiration for these forms of grotesques came from architects who studied in Europe, where they are commonplace. The monster corbels in the lower right are in New York City.

The top row of grotesque half-figures with wings for arms and ornate reptile forms for the lower extremities are from a Los Angeles hotel. They are a popular motif, either as glazed terra-cotta or metal. The middle center panel shows a doorway in Rothenburg above which is an ornamental cartouche flanked by two figures whose lower bodies end in fishtails complete with scales. The lower center panel is a closeup of the female figure. At the bottom left and right panel are two grotesques flanking the tympanum area of an entryway in Rothenburg. They are carved in stone.

From ancient times to the present, half-figures have been popular as the starting point for ornamental detail. The upper part of the human body undergoes little variation from its natural forms. Below the stomach there is an inverted foliage curl from which the bottom scroll ornament grows. Half-figures are found not only in flat panels and bas-relief, but also as corbels, brackets and sculpture in the round. The half-figures act as supports in place of the usual columns.

The half-figure is similar to the caryatid in terms of replacing supporting members, but it is more integrated into the pilaster. The central panel in the top row shows half-figures on an ornate gilded facade in Brussels. The half-figures are transitional ornaments between the spandrel and parapet above. The flanking top images show an unusual group of half-figures in Brussels, with a human mask located below the stomach line. The bottom image showing four half-figures used on a pilaster are in medieval Rothenburg. The bottom right figure protrudes out of a pillar at the corner of a facade in Detroit.

Half-figures have been used in all styles and revival styles and in most countries. A New York City brownstone entrance is graced by a half-figure caryatid. An office building in New York City has a series of four figures similar to the pair shown in the top center panel. The center panel shows a large, carved stone figure located on the window mullion of a residential building in Heidelberg. The far right corner figure supports a balcony in Paris, while the lower figures spring from the pillars to frame an arched opening. The three figures in the bottom center panel frame windows on a facade in Innsbruck.

The Native American Indian was a favorite theme in early turn-of-the-century buildings from coast to coast, and the motifs vary depending on the tribal characteristics of the region. In the Midwest, the motif is often used on columns, in medallions, in panels and on cornices. They appear on many downtown government and commercial office buildings. The images are mostly in a revered form and not representative of the reality of a conquered nation.

A cornice in San Antonio is supported on two large Indian heads. The top right image shows a pilaster capital with an Indian-head motif on a building in Seattle. The Indian heads within the medallions are carved in limestone and appear in the spandrel of an arch on a building in Chicago. The central panel shows a plaque designating a Seattle landmark building in which Indians played a historic part. The bottom center and left panels show a public utility building in Detroit that is rich in Indian inspired ornamentation. The lower right motif is from an office building facade in Kansas City.

"Intaglio" refers to incised carving in which the forms are hollowed out of the surface. It is the reverse of bas-relief, which projects out from the surface. In intaglio carving there is a more subtle relationship between the surface of the build-ing and the carved image or sculpture. Intaglio carving relies on the sun to cast shadows, as does bas-relief sculpture. In some cases this method of sculpture is more dramatic due to the stronger shadows cast by the indentations.

The long frieze at the top is located on a Chicago landmark building. It is a shallow incised relief with an Assyrian influence. The Indian motif appearing next to it is also on a Chicago landmark building. The center images on buildings in Innsbruck are incised in cement plaster. The lower figure of a reaper is carved into the facade of a San Antonio church. The carved image of Neptune and trident is on a panel at a Las Vegas casino. The bottom panel shows incised carving in unpolished granite that is set into a polished granite wall, which emphasizes the carved image, in a New York City building,

The mask was originally an artificial, hollow face, intended to be placed in front of and to conceal the identity of the individual, or to characterize them in some specific manner. The use of masks dates back to the popular harvest games of the earliest Greek period. The masks were transferred to the ancient theater, in which all actors appear in masks. The main classifications were tragedy and comedy. These two motifs are the basic theme for masks since then.

The mouth openings of these masks were unnaturally large and were shaped like a bellmouth, so as to reinforce the voice of the speaker. The masks passed from the theater to mural paintings of theaters and secular facades. The architects of the Renaissance altered the form and put them on keystones of doors and windows and above arches. They appeared in later styles in corbels, and at the perimeter of roof lines. The human face served as the basis for the development of masks, which sometimes combined human and animal characteristics, or human and grotesque characteristics.

It is difficult to distinguish between masks and caricatures, but the French word *mascaron* means "a human face more or less caricaturized." Masks are usually beautiful countenances, either true to nature or idealizing it. Caricatures are deformed images, distorted by accessories or terminating in foliage.

Ancient styles had little use for the ugly and bizarre, while the Middle Ages made frequent use of the grotesque, as superstition and religious beliefs were intermingled. The Renaissance used both, and applied them to keystones, consoles, shields, cartouches, capitals and ornamental panels.

141

The use of metal for ornamental jewelry and coins dates back to antiquity, but its use on buildings was limited to strap ironwork and grilles over openings. The introduction of wrought iron and cast-iron into the vernacular of building materials changed the focus. Craftspeople throughout Europe produced ornamental designs in metal, and these were emulated by architects in America. The use of metal for ornamental details was varied and widespread.

142

Early designs in metal recalled ancient motifs from Egyptian and Greek images on jewelry and coins. These appear mainly in human scale designs over doorways. The top center image is from a doorway in Philadelphia. The right image is from a metal doorway in Augsburg, Germany. The center row shows the use of metal masks along the edge of a cornice. The left example is from a theater in Toronto, and the right image is on an aluminum canopy at the Reynolds Arcade in Rochester. The bottom row shows a doorway at Rockefeller Center in New York with a Botticelli motif.

The doorway of the French Building in New York City is a tour de force in metalwork. It incorporates imagery from Assyrian motifs and combines it with human forms in a modern Art Deco fashion. They are shown in the top and center panels. The bottom center panel shows a figure in cast metal which appears above the entry of a lower Manhattan office building. The motifs are rich and varied, incorporating human and animal forms into a decorative panel. The left and right figures within the octagonal frames are of cast-metal and part of a window guard in New York's Wall Street area.

144

The properties of metal allowed it to be cast, molded or formed. The center image shows two young figures on a metal casting above a doorway in New York City. The cast-metal figure at the left is on a column on a residence in London. The center panel is from a sheet-metal rieze in Boston depicting an abundant harvest. The young boy in the right center panel is found on a glazed metal doorframe on a Boston storefront. The copper sign that appears over a door in San Diego, shows two dancers fashioned in metal. The bottom center image is part of an Art Deco door frame on a Philadelphia building.

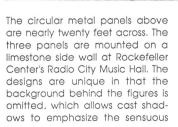

The circular metal panels above are nearly twenty feet across. The three panels are mounted on a limestone side wall at Rockefeller Center's Radio City Music Hall. The designs are unique in that the background behind the figures is omitted, which allows cast shadows to emphasize the sensuous forms. Portions are painted in bright enamel colors, whereas the figures are left in their natural aluminum state. The sculpture on the bottom left appears on a facade in New York City. The one on the right is in old-town Orlando. The center image of workers is from a metal panel over a door in Minneapolis.

FIGURES: NICHE

A niche is a recess in a wall which often contains a statue. Most often niches are semicircular at the back and terminated in a half-dome at the top, sometimes scalloped. Occasionally, small pediments are formed over them, which are supported on consoles. The niche provides a focal point for the statue, and the recess allowed it to be encompassed into the facade. It is a design device that has appeared on facades throughout all classical and revival styles.

The niche was an ornamental device used on the facade to encompass and highlight heroic or symbolic statuary, and the niche itself often attained heroic proportions, as seen in the top left image of a facade in Paris. In the top center panels, the statues in niches are on facades in Brussels, left, and Venice, right. The image on the top right is on a facade in Milan. The two bottom center images are from theaters in New York. The figure on the right is that of the actress Ethel Barrymore. The lower left image shows a female with animal headdress, standing in a niche with a scalloped top shell in New Orleans.

The use of figures to adorn parts of buildings has many variations and applications. There are few that are as unusual as the use of reclining figures. Partially reclined figures are not uncommon, as they fit very handily on the edges and tops of parapets. Here there are many variations, all of which are designed for the particular form of the element, whether it is a regular, broken, curved or angular pediment and whether there are other ornamental elements.

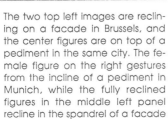

The two top left images are reclining on a facade in Brussels, and the center figures are on top of a pediment in the same city. The female figure on the right gestures from the incline of a pediment in Munich, while the fully reclined figures in the middle left panel recline in the spandrel of a facade in the same city. In the middle right panel, a figure leans on top of a pediment in St. Louis. The reclining family unit rests in the lower corner of a classical pediment on a facade in San Francisco. The reclining figure on the lower right is from a low pediment on a New York City facade.

Sculpture and architecture have been inseparable elements of the world's finest monuments throughout most of history. In some cultures the architecture was almost pure sculpture; in other cultures it was an integrated mix; while at the very least it was applied or affixed to a structure. These sculpted figures were created by a variety of means from carving wood to chiseling marble, incising stone, modeling clay, or casting in metal. The end product was integrated art.

Sculpture appears in front of facades, on the top of facades, and in many places in between. The heroic winged figure with raised sword appears in front of a Renaissance building in Augsburg. The top center panel shows sculpture at the apex of a pediment in Paris. The figure of Columbia, on the top right, is in front of Union Station in Washington, D.C. On the lower left and right panels are sculptures that front the Palais de Chaillot in Paris. The large female figures flanking a cartouche appear over the entrance to a Montreal bank. A cornucopia appears at the feet of one of the sculptures.

The top left angel sounds a horn from the top of a column at Caesar's Palace in Las Vegas. Opposite, a winged maiden raises a crown at the Prince's Gate in Toronto. The center image shows a sculptural trio in front of a Brussels facade. The group of dancing figures in the lower right is adjacent to the main entrance of the Opera House in Paris. The seated figure in the bottom center panel is one of a group of sculptures outside the D'Orsay Museum in Paris. A robust female figure sits in front of a facade in London. The figure at the bottom left sits in front of a government building in St. Louis.

149

Sculptured figures can be created from the most subtle bas-relief or incised forms to sculpture in the round. They can be created in the artist's studio, at the foundry, or at the site. "In situ" sculpture, or that which is in its natural state or origi- nal position, refers to relief panels that are carved on the sides of buildings after the stone has been placed in the wall. The sculptural details of many ancient cultures were fashioned in this manner, from Egyptian temples to Indian stupas.

The bronze female statue in the top center panel stands on top of a pedestal on a facade in Paris, amidst an array of carved orna- mental images. It demonstrates the relationship between the sculpture and architectural elements. The top right image is one of the hun- dreds of sculptures that appear on the facade of the Milan Cathe- dral. The bottom row shows the travertine sculpted reliefs on the fa- cade of a building in Los Angeles. The panels portray three builders; Hiram, Sir Christopher Wren, and Thomas Jefferson, whose image also appears on the facade of the Los Angeles County Courthouse.

The use of free-standing sculpture in courtyards and as frontispieces for new buildings is rapidly gaining use once again. It was inconceivable to design a classical building without ornamental detail, sculpture and free-standing statuary around it. However, modernism did away with the need altogether. Fortunately, many architects and owners today are including free-standing sculpture in plaza areas, and are using both classical and modern themes as their inspiration.

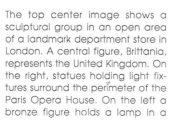

The top center image shows a sculptural group in an open area of a landmark department store in London. A central figure, Brittania, represents the United Kingdom. On the right, statues holding light fixtures surround the perimeter of the Paris Opera House. On the left a bronze figure holds a lamp in a renovated Georgetown building. On the bottom center are cast-metal figures holding globes in the courtyard of Worldwide Plaza in New York City. The lower left shows the trident-bearing figure in front of the Postmodern Portland Building. The right figure is in the entrance courtyard of an Atlanta highrise.

151

There are many human figures with wings among the ornamental motifs found on building facades. These include winged cherubs, grotesques, angels and other faces. The use of winged figures appear early in Assyria and Greece, and the Romans used the device and passed it on to the Renaissance and revival styles. The winged angel was used extensively on Christian structures, but the use of the winged figure continued past its use as a religious icon.

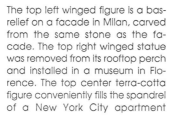

The top left winged figure is a bas-relief on a facade in Milan, carved from the same stone as the facade. The top right winged statue was removed from its rooftop perch and installed in a museum in Florence. The top center terra-cotta figure conveniently fills the spandrel of a New York City apartment house. The center three horizontal panels show the use of wings on angels, griffins, and cherubs. The lower left image of the angel is on a New York City church. The angel on the right is in the Art Institute of Chicago. It was one of twenty figures at the parapet of a demolished Chicago building.

FRESCO

A fresco is a mural painting in which colors are applied to fresh lime plaster while it is still wet. The water-based colors unite with the plaster base and become an integral part of its surface. Retouching or highlighting is usually done after the plaster is dry. Although fresco painting is usually associated with interior murals like Michelangelo's Sistine Chapel ceiling, it was also used during the Renaissance and later periods to apply ornamental motifs to building facades.

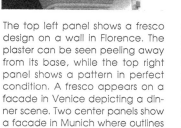

The top left panel shows a fresco design on a wall in Florence. The plaster can be seen peeling away from its base, while the top right panel shows a pattern in perfect condition. A fresco appears on a facade in Venice depicting a dinner scene. Two center panels show a facade in Munich where outlines of the architectural details are painted on the surface. The right center panel indicates how the corner quoins and window trim are painted on a facade in Innsbruck. Ornate window trim is painted on the surface of a facade, while In Bavarian villages entire facades are painted with ornamentation.

153

FRIEZE

A frieze is a continuous elevated horizontal ornamental band or panel usually executed below the cornice or above an entryway. It is the middle section of the entablature, which originally consisted of a series of alternating triglyphs and metopes. This section of the entablature was the favorite location for bas-relief sculpture, replacing the triglyphs. Friezes were executed in bas-relief, intaglio, and high-relief sculpture, featuring the use of realistic and symbolic imagery.

154

The top frieze appears above the entryway on the Buffalo City Hall. Scenes of industry and agriculture are typical on this type of low-relief frieze. The high-relief frieze below it is under a cornice on a building in Chicago. In the left middle panel, a frieze of incised figures showing Assyrian and Greek influences, appears above the windows of a retail store in San Diego. The right panel, on the cornice of the Art Institute in Chicago, recalls themes from classical Greece. The frieze on the lower left appears on the Montreal Musuem of Fine Art, and the right frieze is over an entrance to a government complex in London.

155

The top row shows a frieze in high relief on a building in New York City where strong shadows define the forms. The shallow relief in the center panel is from a facade rich in ornamentation, in Boston . A male face appears on the corner of a frieze on a Renaissance facade in Florence. The long horizontal frieze in the left center panel shows cherubs in a garden landscape on a building in Brussels. The opposite panel shows two family groups flanking a central symbolic ffigure, on a Kansas City facade. The bottom row of figures appear on the facade of the New York studio of the painter Gainsborough.

The gable is the entire end wall of a building above the level of the eaves. The top conforms to the slope of the roof which abuts against it. Sometimes it has a series of steps up the sides, or it may be curved or shaped like scrolls, which are called fractables. Fractables involve the coping on the gable wall of a building when carried above the roof, especially when broken into steps or curves forming an ornamental silhouette on the top of the facade.

A figure emerges from an ornamental balcony on a gable in Munich. The top center gable shows two human heads. The left one has a bandaged head and pained expression, whereas the right one smiles with the tooth removed. The middle row shows typical gables: the two on the left are in Rothenburg, the right one in Heidelberg. The stepped gable is typical of those in Munich, and the sinuous roof with ornamental gable is in Augsburg. Ornamental metal caps gables in Rothenburg, and gables in the bottom row show intricate wood patterns in Cape May and Victorian designs in San Francisco.

The builders of the Middle Ages had an ingenious device to shed water from the roofs of structures. It was a long horizontal projecting spout which discharged the water clear of the walls. The spout was in the form of a lion's head or other creature, with the water flowing through the mouth or other orifices of the body. In ecclesiastical architecture they are called gargoyles, and were mostly carved of stone. In dwellings they were sometimes made of ornamental metal.

The gargoyles of Notre Dame are certainly the most well-known, and are seen in the top left and center panels. They form a continuous ring around the upper level of the cathedral. Other forms were used for gargoyles, such as human and animal heads, and appeared on many medieval churches, particularly in France. Many of the images shown here are in the archeological exhibit at the Palais de Chaillot in Paris. The bottom left and center panels show gargoyles on the Town Hall in Brussel's Grand-Place, whose facade also contains hundreds of statues of prominent citizens of the city.

157

KEYSTONE

The keystone is the central or uppermost wedge-shaped stone in an arch, which completes it and locks its members together. It is often embellished with ornamentation. The remaining external faces of the arch usually remain unadorned. Human faces, angels, animals, plants, and abstract patterns appear as ornamental motifs. Keystones are usually made of the same material as the rest of the facade, such as brownstone, limestone, terra-cotta or cast iron.

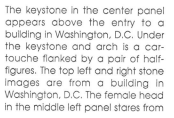

The keystone in the center panel appears above the entry to a building in Washington, D.C. Under the keystone and arch is a cartouche flanked by a pair of half-figures. The top left and right stone images are from a building in Washington, D.C. The female head in the middle left panel stares from above a window in Paris. The Indian motif gazes from a doorway in Philadelphia. The bottom left image looks down from a door in a New York City brownstone, and the stony stare of the female on the right is from a doorway in Munich. The figure in the bottom smiles from beneath a balcony.

The female in the top center panel smiles from above a Paris window. The two flanking top panels show grotesque images in keystones; the left from above a window in the County Courthouse in Des Moines, and the right above a doorway in Munich. In the two center panels, a bearded face is flanked by two grotesques, and two antic creatures appear over arched windows in Heidelberg. The left middle image catches a worried look on the female's face. Two Art Deco faces gaze sternly from above arched windows in San Diego. The bottom center panel shows a terra-cotta keystone on a New York theater.

159

160

The top center panel shows an ornamental keystone in a brick facade in New York City. The two top flanking panels show helmeted female figures above a scroll. The left one is in Washington D.C., and the right one on a classical facade in Toronto. Natural vegetation is often combined with the human face as in the left and right center images. The double-headed keystone in the center appears on a facade in Heidelberg. The bottom center image shows a female head in an articulated brick facade in New York City. The lower right figure is one of the very few profiles among keystone images.

A label stop is the termination of a hood-molding or arched dripstone that occurs over doors and sometimes over windows. The lower ends of the molding terminate with a face or a grotesque figure, from which the water runoff will drip.

These slightly projecting areas are formed over arches and near openings to direct and shed water from the wall above. The label stop is usually fashioned from the same material as the facade wall on which it appears.

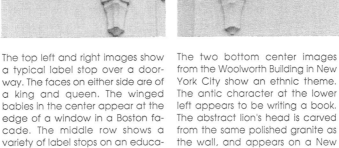

The top left and right images show a typical label stop over a doorway. The faces on either side are of a king and queen. The winged babies in the center appear at the edge of a window in a Boston facade. The middle row shows a variety of label stops on an educational building in New York City.

The two bottom center images from the Woolworth Building in New York City show an ethnic theme. The antic character at the lower left appears to be writing a book. The abstract lion's head is carved from the same polished granite as the wall, and appears on a New York City building.

The medallion is an ornamental device, within which an object is represented in relief. These objects usually involve a figure, head, or floral design. The medallion is applied or incised into a wall, frieze, or other architectural member. They are usually centralized and isolated, but are found most frequently in the spandrel segment of arches, where they have been used since ancient times. Medallions can be any size or shape, circular, hexagonal, or oval.

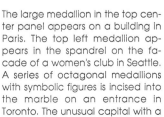

The large medallion in the top center panel appears on a building in Paris. The top left medallion appears in the spandrel on the facade of a women's club in Seattle. A series of octagonal medallions with symbolic figures is incised into the marble on an entrance in Toronto. The unusual capital with a coinlike medallion within the center of the Ionic-style capital has the name of the company inscribed on it. In the bottom panels, large medallions are carved in a limestone wall, with symbolic figures carved within, and medallions appear above bas-reliefs on New York's Municipal Building.

The top center medallion features an aquatic theme, with young maidens flanked by marine life, on the Atlantic City Convention Center, home of the American beauty pageant. The top left and right images appear on an ornamented stucco facade in Heidelberg. The oval medallions in the middle row appear on a department store facade in the same city. The large medallion in the bottom panel appears between the windows of an apartment house in Paris. The lower right image is one of a pair above an entrance and the lower left image appears on a door panel, both in New York City.

PANEL

A panel consists of a flat surface, often sunken or recessed below the surrounding area, distinctly set off by moldings or some other decorative device. Panel ornamentation is designed for a definite, bounded space, so that it fits into that space alone. Panels are found in many of the following shapes: rectangular, circular, elliptical, polygonal, triangular, or any combination. Geometric, natural, or artificial forms may be used to fill the panel, and half-figures are often included.

Designs within panels tend to be symmetrical about either the vertical or horizontal axis, but there is no specific formula. Panel designs were popular during the Baroque Revival styles, as the florid ornamentation was easily applied to the panel format. Faces and figures are generally intertwined within the ornamentation. The large face in the top center panel appears on a stucco facade in Los Angeles. The panel designs in the middle row are all of cast metal. The left and right panels are terracotta, and the bottom center design appears on a New York City theater building.

PARAPET

Parapets occur at the edge of raised platforms, terraces, bridges, and above cornices. There are many forms of the parapet, which is the extension of the wall plane above the roof line. They consist of rows of balusters, pierced or perforated stone or wood railings, or cast- or wrought-iron railings. Parapets of perforated wood, typical of Swiss architecture, feature vertical boards with cutouts. The patterns created by negative spaces are as important as the solid ones.

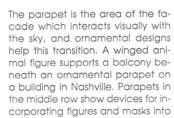

The parapet is the area of the facade which interacts visually with the sky, and ornamental designs help this transition. A winged animal figure supports a balcony beneath an ornamental parapet on a building in Nashville. Parapets in the middle row show devices for incorporating figures and masks into the parapet area. In the bottom center panel faces appear amid baroque ornament in a Santa Monica commercial building. The modern-looking parapet in the lower left is on a Renaissance facade in Venice, and the far right panel is an Art Deco design on a commercial facade in Oakland.

A pediment is a low-pitched triangular gable above the wall of a facade or a smaller element above a door or window. Pediments are often broken open at the top, and the gap is often filled with a cartouche or other ornament. Pediments can also be curved, and they can be enclosed or open in either mode. The pediment was a favorite place for sculpture enclosed within the form, as part of broken pediments, or on top as statuary.

166

The center panel shows a sculptural group within a pediment of a classical structure in San Francisco. The broken scroll pediments in the top right panel are on the entry facade of the Freedom Tower in Miami. The curved pediment in the left middle row is at the top of a facade in Augsburg, and figures rest on top of pediments in the center panels. The right image is a series of broken pediments around a circular window in the upper stories of the Louvre in Paris. The broken pediment at the bottom encompasses a baby's head. The lower right articulated pediment is at the top of a facade in Brussels.

PILASTER

The pilaster is a partial pier or column projecting from a flat wall or facade of a building and treated like a column, often with a base and capital. The pilaster, unlike some columns, does not usually taper upwards; if it does taper, or-namentation is usually avoided. Ornamentation usually takes the form of elongated, sunken panels which are bordered by moldings. Designs may consist of festoons of flowers, trophies, or human figures combined with these elements.

Florid pilaster capitals and abstract tile designs highlight this commercial facade in Detroit. On the left a face appears on top of a pilaster capital above a Paris doorway. On the top right the brick pilaster with recessed slots terminates with a large human face within the capital on a New York City apartment building. The helmeted figures in the bifront capital sits on top of a pilaster between windows in a San Francisco facade. The large face and ornamental foliage appear within the capital on a renovated New York City building. The lower left and center panel are pliasters on a New York theater.

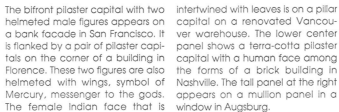

168

The bifront pilaster capital with two helmeted male figures appears on a bank facade in San Francisco. It is flanked by a pair of pilaster capitals on the corner of a building in Florence. These two figures are also helmeted with wings, symbol of Mercury, messenger to the gods. The female Indian face that is intertwined with leaves is on a pillar capital on a renovated Vancouver warehouse. The lower center panel shows a terra-cotta pilaster capital with a human face among the forms of a brick building in Nashville. The tall panel at the right appears on a mullion panel in a window in Augsburg.

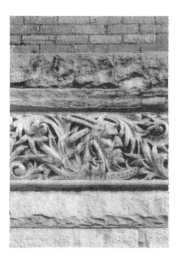

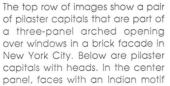

The top row of images show a pair of pilaster capitals that are part of a three-panel arched opening over windows in a brick facade in New York City. Below are pilaster capitals with heads. In the center panel, faces with an Indian motif appear above the pilaster capital on a travertine-faced facade in Miami Beach. The two flanking panels show pilasters with Indian-head themes from a renovated warehouse building in Vancouver's Gaslight Square.

PLAQUE

A plaque is a flat plate, slab or disk that is often inscribed and added to or set into a panel on a wall. The plaque is usually self-contained within a panel and oftentimes contains a title or slogan at the bottom of the plaque. The shape of a plaque can be oval, circular, or in the shape of a shield, which it often resembles. The inside of the plaque can contain symbols, images of figures, words, or a combination of all three. The plaque has been used throughout all styles.

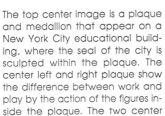

The top center image is a plaque and medallion that appear on a New York City educational building, where the seal of the city is sculpted within the plaque. The center left and right plaque show the difference between work and play by the action of the figures inside the plaque. The two center panels are located on a municipal building in Chicago and feature the seal of the city flanked by bas-relief figures. The two bottom images are from an Immigraqtions building in New York City, and features a series of plaques around the lower story. Each plaque features the symbol of a country.

SIGNS

Building signs are important devices, not only for identification purposes, but also to give directions and for advertising as well. Early signs were decorative and integrated into the facade ornamentation rather than merely be-ing applied to it. Signs were symbolic of the trade and applied to the facade in plaques and as carvings in spandrel panels. Signs in small villages and towns were usually coordinated using similar ornamental motifs and materials.

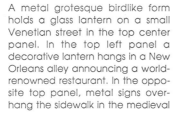

A metal grotesque birdlike form holds a glass lantern on a small Venetian street in the top center panel. In the top left panel a decorative lantern hangs in a New Orleans alley announcing a world-renowned restaurant. In the opposite top panel, metal signs overhang the sidewalk in the medieval town of Rothenburg. The Art Deco Victory theater in Vancouver displays the profile of a female. In San Francisco, a children's toy store features a comic animal. In the bottom center panel a sign is embedded in the masonry wall of a Venetian bank. The grotesque mask holds an inscribed plaque.

SOFFIT

The soffit consists of the exposed underneath surface of balconies, doorways, beams, lintels, cornices, archways or bay windows. It was a favorite place for ornamentation since it was exposed to view whenever people looked up at a facade. The primary location for ornamentation was above doors, and, as these items were related to human scale, the faces of humans were mostly used. On the underside of balconies and bay windows larger-scale designs were used.

The cartouche and face at the top center appears on a theater tower in Detroit. The top left lion's head appears over a residential doorway in London. The top right figure poking out beneath a soffit, is in Rothenburg. The grim face in the left middle panel is under a bay in a New York brownstone. The floral design in concrete with an Art Nouveau flavor is on the soffit of a balcony in Innsbruck. The bearded figure appears under a New York City balcony, and the baroque forms are under a balcony on a San Francisco residence. The bottom carved figure appears in the soffit of a New York City doorway.

SPANDREL

The spandrel of a facade has two definitions. One refers to the space between the top of a floor and the window sill of the floor above. It is also the space between converging sides of arches. The rectangular spandrel has been a favorite location for ornamentation since medieval times. Designs consisted of decorative medallions, human faces, cartouches and ornamental panels. The practice continues today, as the rectangular form of spandrel is now more prevalent.

173

The bearded and helmeted face appears in the spandrel area of a residential facade in Munich, as seen in the top center panel. The flanking left and right images are in the spandrels on structures in the Grand-Place in Brussels. The long horizontal panels in the center are typical of those seen on the wide bays under windows of brownstones in New York City. The bottom left image is a design in cast-iron that features a female face along with festoons and other figures on a facade in New York's theater district. The bottom left female face with wings appears on a residential facade in Munich.

SPANDREL

The more traditional definition of a spandrel relates to the triangular space formed between the curved sides of adjacent arches and the horizontal line across their top. This space originated during the Roman era with the development of the arch, and was used over doors and windows. This area became decorated with figures, though it was an awkward shape to fill. The device most often used involved semi-reclining figures with wings or trumpets to fill the space.

174

The top center panel identifies the spandrel area of a building in Philadelphia, which includes not only religious but social organizations in the figures and medallions that surround it. The flanking top panels show figures holding symbolic images on a Chicago courthouse. The middle panel shows designs from structures in Paris on the left, and Philadelphia's City Hall on the right. The lower center panel shows a terra-cotta carving in a rusticated brownstone spandrel on a New York commercial building. The right image shows a stone spandrel with female head set into a smooth stone wall for emphasis.

It is unusual to see the figures break out of the spandrel frame, but this does occur in the spandrel design of a building in Philadelphia, as can be seen in the center panel. In the top right the winged figure with a trumpet fills the spandrel area on the Arc de Triomphe in Paris. At the bottom left a tall panel shows a winged female figure holding a mask on a theater facade in New York's Times Square. On the lower right a half-figure fills the space with naturalistic tendrils in Detroit. The bottom center panel shows one-half of the spandrel on the facade of the Marble Arch near London's Hyde Park.

SYMBOLS

It was the custom of the Greeks to hang the weapons that the fleeing enemy left behind on the trunks of trees. These tokens of victory, or trophies, have also found a place in ornamentation. The Romans erected artificial symbolic trophies in the form of monuments and triumphal arches. Since then, trophies have been used to decorate all monuments connected with battle and victory. The ornaments have been used in friezes, pilasters, and ornamental panels.

The telephone frieze appears on the utilities office building in Cincinnati along with a bas-relief of Mercury, symbolizing communications. The top left and right medallions show a fine-arts theme on a New York City building. In the center, a frieze of musical instruments runs around the top of a university building in Cincinnati. The lower left panel shows symbols within a metal plaque on a building in New York's theater district, and a similar panel is seen at the right. A plaque and symbol clearly relate to music as the winged cherub presides over a musical score on the facade of a New York City building.

Tools and instruments were used in a symbolic form as ornamentation in panels and friezes. Singing is symbolized by the lyre, for example; music by violins, horns, and pipes; and dancing by the tambourine. Acting is symbolized by masks; painting by the brush and palette; sculpture by the hammer and chisel; and architecture by the square, straightedge and compass. Trade is represented by casks and bales of goods; agriculture by the plow and scythe.

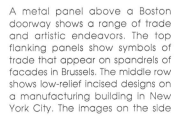

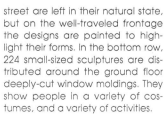

A metal panel above a Boston doorway shows a range of trade and artistic endeavors. The top flanking panels show symbols of trade that appear on spandrels of facades in Brussels. The middle row shows low-relief incised designs on a manufacturing building in New York City. The images on the side street are left in their natural state, but on the well-traveled frontage the designs are painted to highlight their forms. In the bottom row, 224 small-sized sculptures are distributed around the ground floor deeply-cut window moldings. They show people in a variety of costumes, and a variety of activities.

177

TYMPANUM

The tympanum is the triangular space between the horizontal and sloping cornices or the arched cornice immediately above the opening of a doorway. It often contains sculptured figures or cartouches. In medieval times figures were used extensively to fill this area, including human bodies with serpentlike tails. Later periods used more naturalistic human figures. It has always been an area to receive ornamental treatment from medieval times to today.

178

The figures above the doorway in the top center panel are on a restaurant in Dinklesbuhl and combine human characters and animal forms. On the Bank of Montreal the classical tympanum in the right center panel has overlooked the typical classical motif in favor of one more in keeping with the frontier image. In the lower left panel the curved tympanum of the Chicago Civic Theater and Opera House features two reclining figures with a pair of theater masks. The carved wooden face and ornament in the lower right panel are one of a pair above an arched doorway in Florence.

179

The top center panel shows ornamental scrolls and scalloped shell above the eaves of a New York City building. The flanking left and right figures are above the doorways in medieval Rothenburg. The left middle panel shows a female head inside a medallion within the arched tympanum of a New York City apartment building. It is set within a field of ceramic tile. In the right panel, two sculptured figures rest over a doorway in a New York City office building. The bottom left and center panels shows the use of sculptured figures, centaurs and symbols on a Parisian structure. The right image is a dormer in Paris.

A window is an exterior wall opening, usually glazed, which admits light, if fixed, and air if operable. An elegant form of circular window was popular in the Gothic period. consisting of a circular stone frame with carved stone mullions radiating towards the center like the spokes of a wheel. The spaces between were filled with colorful designs using stained glass. The circular window has remained a favorite design element in terms of the use of ornamental faces and figures.

The double figures flanking each side of the circular window appears on a classical Boston facade. The center image with the large grinning face is on a theater building in New York City. The right middle panel shows a pair of female figures surrounding a large circular window on a facade in Brussels. The circular corner window features a face mask within a broken pediment on a theater building in New York City. The window at the bottom left panel designed like the stern of a ship appears on the facade of the Mariner's Club in New York City; the ram's head from the window appears on the right.

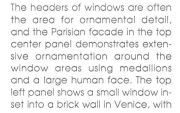

The headers of windows are often the area for ornamental detail, and the Parisian facade in the top center panel demonstrates extensive ornamentation around the window areas using medallions and a large human face. The top left panel shows a small window inset into a brick wall in Venice, with a winged cherub head both under and over the rectangular window. The lower left panel shows an Indian motif applied to the face that appears over the window at the old U.S. Customs House in New York City. The middle right panel is from an Art Nouveau gable above a pair of windows in Paris.

RENOVATION

The reclaiming of old buildings for continuing use has become an important element in architectural practice and construction activity. Whether it is called renovation, rehabilitation, restoration, reuse, recycling or some other term, we have given this activity a new place in our vocabulary of building terminology. Renovation practices are now desirable, not only for historic and humanistic reasons, but for the aesthetic values and character that older buildings offer. They are the major ways of preserving our architectural heritage. The buildings that exist in every community are overlooked and oftentimes unappreciated. In their day, many of these buildings were not necessarily significant, either in function or appearance. They were working buildings built for a utilitarian purpose. Today, they are important to us to a degree that would surprise the original owners and builders. Their scale, character and ornamental detail are the very qualities that we lack in our environment.

Renovation of old buildings for residential use is on the increase. Some of these buildings are significant relics of the past; some are simple structures for everyday use: barns, carriage houses, and firehouses. The reuse of these structures can keep the scale of neighborhoods intact. Warehouses. lofts and factory buildings are also relics of a bygone era, abandoned when a changing technology made them obsolete. Many have been converted to new commercial and office uses. Since such buildings are frequently found in clusters in one section of a city, the renovation of one often leads to the revitalization of the whole area. There are countless examples throughout the country. The vast interior space that is typical of this type of structure makes it very suitable for redesign to meet the needs of almost any kind of business or commercial use. The economic advantage of renovating these structures is one of the factors contributing to its wide acceptance. The transformation of an old warehouse or factory into a colorful collection of shops and restaurants is perhaps one of the most wide spread trends today.

Most cities have a reservoir of old and obsolete buildings that are situated in very desirable locations. They can be converted to civic and public uses, such as arts centers, cinemas, or other community functions. Some fortunate cities still have theaters that reflect the golden era of the stage and screen. Many of these are preserved, and again serve in their original function. Many public buildings, such as museums and libraries, have also been restored to their original glory. In many cases this applies not only to the architectural space, but to artwork, mosaics and murals on ceilings and walls. Restoring these period pieces requires a special kind of concern. Every detail must be respected, not only for its current use, but for those of another design era. The first step in restoring these structures is to save them from whatever threatened it in the first place.

Preservation, restoration, reconstruction, renovation, remodeling, reuse; these terms are used so often that we ought to define them, though there is often an overlap in practice. Remodeling and reuse involve changing the basic structure or design of a building. Remodeling involves removing existing components and redesigning something new for the same space. Preservation means keeping something the way it always was; restoration means putting it back into its original condition. Restoration technically means returning a structure to a certain time, usually to its original appearance. Since authenticity is the primary goal, it calls for extensive research. Restoration is frequently restricted to structures intended for public use, or those opened as architectural or historic house museums. Reconstruction means remaking or copying the existing forms in the same or new materials. It is rebuilding what has been lost, usually starting from the ground up. Often it is difficult to determine what is old and what is new in reconstructions, and this may or may not be an important issue. Adaptive reuse of old buildings is especially challenging, but the results are not only economically but alsoaesthetically rewarding.

When confronted with a choice, the public is becoming more prone to protest demolition of favorite buildings and to show appreciation for responsible restorations. Fifty-five thousand San Franciscans signed petitions against the proposed destruction of the City of Paris department store, owned by Neiman Marcus. The president of the Merchants National Bank in Winona, Minnesota, was surprised when citizens reacted negatively to the bank's plan to replace the 1912 Louis Sullivan version. They restored the old bank instead of building the planned new one. The bank was rewarded with commendations, streams of visitors, and even transferrals of funds from competing banks by appreciative members of the community. The Cleveland Trust Company was threatened with removal of substantial accounts if they tore down their turn-of-the-century Neoclassical headquarters. The Rookery in Chicago, the Chandler Building in Atlanta, and the Academy of Music and Pennsylvania Academy of Fine Arts in Philadelphia have all been restored and modernized. Carnegie Hall in New York City, which was nearly torn down when its replacement was built in Lincoln Center, is engaged by many performers who prefer it to its replacement.

Adaptive reuse is an answer that makes good economic sense. A national restaurant chain is based on the use of old railroad cars; banks and churches have been successfully converted to restaurants. A block of nineteenth-century buildings, left behind when the street was raised in Atlanta, now houses cafes and shops in Underground Atlanta. Classic reuse projects like Ghirardelli Square and the Cannery in San Francisco have had an important impact on other projects throughout the nation, such as the development of Georgetown in Washington, D.C. There are countless others inspired by the same projects; Larimer Square in Denver, Pioneer Square in Seattle, Trolley Square in Salt Lake City, Canal Square in Georgetown, and Gaslight Square in Vancouver, B.C.

More and more old buildings that would have been demolished a decade ago are being adapted to serve new purposes. They are a resource that represent materials, techniques, styles and artwork that we will never see again. They are truly monumental works of art and architecture, and their destruction would represent a very significant loss which we could never again recover.

FACADE

These images represents a project undertaken over thirty years ago as a reaction to the prevailing policies that placed many of the finest examples of Victorian architecture in jeopardy. Not only would the ornament be lost forever, but entire facades would be destroyed, not to mention the lives that went on behind these facades. While buildings were being razed, I was preserving them photographically for a book called *FACADE: Changing Face of a City.*

At the same time a professor at MIT had published a book titled *The Federal Bulldozer.* Its impact was as strong as its message: " By the end of 1965 approximately 900,000 people had lost their homes. Almost 50,000 businesses had been forced to close their doors; one-fourth of them will never open again. An area of land more than two times that of Manhattan had been reduced to rubble. This was not the result of an atomic attack. This is an actual account of destruction brought about in the name of the 'public interest,' under a federal government program known as urban renewal."

Urban renewal began with the Housing Act of 1949, Professor Martin Anderson explained, its goal is to eliminate slums and blighted areas, and to stimulate housing growth. As of 1962, 636 American cities were involved in 1,210 urban renewal projects. The program destroyed over 126,000 dwelling units, 25,000 of them in good condition, and added only 28,000 new units to the housing supply; more than four times as many homes were destroyed as were built. During the same period of time, private enterprise increased the supply of dwelling units by over eighteen million, a 63% gain in one decade.

188 The problems associated with urban renewal became front page news, and Anderson's book became the standard bearer. He pointed out that the cost of relocation, and disruption of family life and business is direct and tangible. The benefits of urban renewal are for most communities symbolic and intangible. His final suggestion was that the federal urban renewal program be repealed and that no new projects be authorized. In the five years that followed, over seventy cities from coast to coast rejected urban renewal projects.

This project covered an area of 28 city blocks, and while undergoing redevelopment acquired the appearance of a demolished city. When the dust settled, not a single building remained. Numerous local articles debated the issue on both sides while it was happening, but no one wrote any books about the replacement buildings. Fortunately, this program was never repeated in this city, and the term "urban renewal" is something that will have to be described and defined for our grandchildren, because it is no longer in our vocabulary.

The stone and terra-cotta faces and figures on older buildings, mounted on facades, over keystones, supporting window lintels, on medallions and entry soffits have been where they are for over half a century. We have been too busy to notice them, or we fail to look up from the street to see them, until we find them being destroyed. Then they stand out, not as evidence of the "good old days," but as harbingers and omens of a vanishing environment.

Various individuals and groups have formed organizations to call attention to this loss of our architectural heritage. One is the Anonymous Arts Recovery Society, a tax-exempt, non-profit organization devoted to the salvage of carvings, sculptures, bas-reliefs, and other ornamentation. Most examples are classic representations, such as caryatids and minor gods. Some are representative of particular personages, popular figures of the day, but their identities are for the most part completely forgotten. There are also many other salvage shops that offer these carved stone items for sale.

What is most significant about the Anonymous Arts Recovery Society is the final resting place for these special pieces. They are in a specially designed sculpture garden at the Brooklyn Museum. Along with the most humble garlanded cupid will be an historic piece like the capitals rescued from the fa-cade of Louis Sullivan's Bayard Building. It is an outdoor garden, so the pieces can be viewed in natural light. However, they are laid out like tombstones in the ivy covered ground. Here they will stay as constant reminders of a time of architectural ornamentation that we are not likely to ever witness again.

This project represents a personal adventure in salvage that shaped many of the concepts in this book. While photographing the destruction of San Francisco's Victorian buildings, I wandered into this church, which sat clearly in the path of destruction, along with my friend and associate, Fred Stitt. We were both young architects, and we took on the task of saving this beautiful Gothic redwood roof from the wrecker's ball without any financial means of accomplishing it.

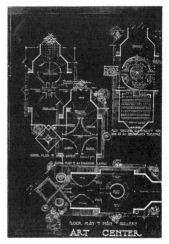

Rescued Church Roof to Shelter Arts

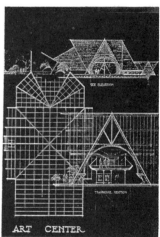

The secret lay in creating a public interest story, and getting the community involved in a worthy project. No less than a dozen stories appeared in the local papers outlining the case and seeking support. The public support was encouraging. By the deadline, enough money was raised to pay for the careful dismantling of the roof. Plans were drawn up for its new use as an Art Center. These drawings were exhibited at local art fairs, in galleries, but most importantly in the local newspapers.. Without the media support the public would not have known about this project at all.

HIGHWAY TABERNACLE CHURCH

A fire ravaged the main sanctuary of the Highway Tabernacle church in Philadelphia, leaving behind a charred ruin. The church, erected over one hundred twenty years ago, appeared to be damaged beyond repair. Research was undertaken by Wiss, Janney, Elstner to determine the church's structural and architectural history. It was found that in addition to the fire, previous renovations had severely compromised the structural integrity of the main sanctuary roof.

Falling debris caused the balcony to collapse and the columns to tilt dangerously. The structural system of the sanctuary roof was characterized by wood scissor trusses. The lower chords of the trusses are arched rather than straight. Wood tracery filled the open web spaces. The cast-iron columns, installed in an earlier renovation, carried the vertical loads. New timber members with bolted steel plate connections strengthened the reconstructed trusses. The original ceiling was decorated with frescoed plaster and carved wooden trim, and all decorative wood members were repaired or replaced.

Around the world individuals are erecting scaffolding as a vital part of restoration projects. At Ankor Wat in Cambodia the scaffolding is made of bamboo. In Venice it is supported on boats. We are accustomed to seeing scaffolding everywhere we look. Some have claimed that the Pompidou Center in Paris is a permanent homage to temporary scaffolding. The main function of scaffolding is to provide a level working surface, but it is camouflage as well.

The center image shows how a totally sheathed building in London becomes a non-facade. The flanking images show the aesthetic advantages of symmetrical scaffolding. The middle row shows a Renaissance doorway in Florence protected from its neighbor's renovation. Workers balance on a floating scaffold in Venice, and the Pitti Palace in Florence gets a cleaning. Slender scaffolding and gothic tracery are visually compatible. The constant renovation going on in Rothenburg preserves its medieval character. The bottom center screen shows images of the hidden architectural features.

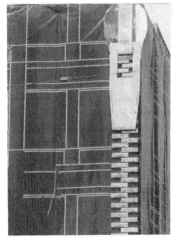

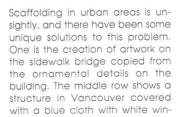

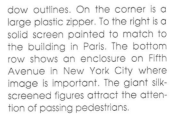

Scaffolding in urban areas is unsightly, and there have been some unique solutions to this problem. One is the creation of artwork on the sidewalk bridge copied from the ornamental details on the building. The middle row shows a structure in Vancouver covered with a blue cloth with white window outlines. On the corner is a large plastic zipper. To the right is a solid screen painted to match to the building in Paris. The bottom row shows an enclosure on Fifth Avenue in New York City where image is important. The giant silk-screened figures attract the attention of passing pedestrians.

The Carnegie is one of Pittsburgh's most important landmarks, and comprises a museum of art, a museum of natural history, a music hall, and a library. The Italian Renaissance sandstone structure had been enlarged to four times its size in the Beaux-Arts style. Cleaning it's dirty masonry produced dramatic changes. Many think cleaning is an end in itself, but the removal of dirt encrustations alone is an act of preservation much more important than the resultant appearance.

The initial task of Williams Trebilcock Whitehead, architects, was to understand the nature of the masonry and how it might best be cleaned. Various methods were tested, and for most areas a two-step chemical cleaning process was sufficient to remove the century of atmospheric pollutants. In some areas, black encrustation was impervious to the chemicals and had to be cleaned with abrasives. A silica-sand water/grit process removed the encrustation without any damage, and the chemical cleaning process finished the job. The architectural details were once again visible.

Another world-renowned museum, the Louvre in Paris, also suffered from years of neglect of its richly ornamented facades. Dirt and grime had accumulated on its stone surface to the point where ornamentation appeared blackened beyond recognition. When the Grand Louvre project was initiated, with its pristine pyramid, it became necessary to bring the old building facades up to the standards of the new. The delicate glass pyramid was designed to complement the solid facades, which would be highly visible from inside the new area. Restoration of the sculpture was undertaken at the same time.

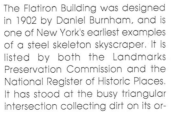

The Flatiron Building was designed in 1902 by Daniel Burnham, and is one of New York's earliest examples of a steel skeleton skyscraper. It is listed by both the Landmarks Preservation Commission and the National Register of Historic Places. It has stood at the busy triangular intersection collecting dirt on its ornamental stone and carved details. Among its features are the large female medusa-like faces within circular wreaths that ring the lower level. The exterior has been steam-cleaned and the joints in the stone have been repointed. Much of the detail has been restored and the lobby renovated.

197

Designed by Louis Sullivan in 1895, the once-grand building in Buffalo, New York, had fallen into disrepair over the years through neglect and alterations. The thirteen-story structure, once the nation's second skyscraper, had achieved National Historic Landmark status in 1973. A fire in 1975 forced the closing of the building. In 1977, despite its landmark status, Buffalo watched with indifference as what may be Sullivan's greatest commercial building, slip into emptiness and dereliction.

198

A task force of community leaders, architects, engineers, and real estate advisors guided the landmark back to its original pre-eminent stature. The requirements faced by Cannon, the restoration architects, was that the building be brought up to modern codes and standards. They had to interweave historic spaces with modern mechanical, electrical, and plumbing systems. Much of the terra-cotta surface was in need of repair, and the joints were raked and re-pointed with a mortar that was colored to match the original. The terra-cotta surface was used both for decoration and fireproofing.

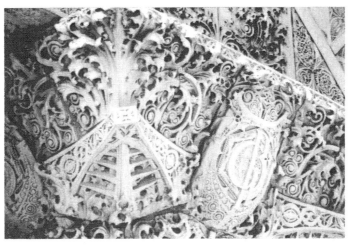

The terra-cotta was blackened beyond recognition, and it was cleaned with chemicals and low-pressure water hoses. The entire facade is clad in terra-cotta ornamental panels. Many of these panels were damaged, and five-hundred pieces were recast in fourteen different shapes. Louis Sulli-van's ornament is so sensitively designed and intricately detailed that the closer one looks at the carvings the more one finds. In addition to preserving the past, the building was brought up to modern standards and functions once again as prime office space. The building has won many awards.

Small-scale restoration and renovation are an important part of preserving the fabric of our commercial street frontage. Many of the structures in New York's Union Square were designed for much different uses a hundred years ago.

Since that time, merchants have modified and in many cases destroyed the original ornamentation. Sometimes historic research is required to find evidence of the original design. In some cases, fragments may still be available.

200

This ornate structure had been modified so many times at the entry level that only fragments of the original ornamentation were left. However, it was enough to cast latex molds to re-create the ornamental patterns. Once the initial pieces were cast, they were installed and the reconstruction begun. Fortunately, there are still craftspeople who understand ornamental detail. It is a hand operation which begins with the mixing of the special mortar on site and sculpting of the detail with special tools. Refinements can be made with sharp chisels and the final result finished with sandpaper.

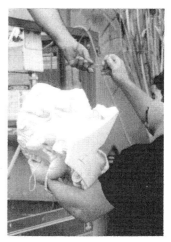

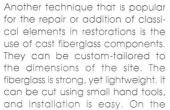

Another technique that is popular for the repair or addition of classical elements in restorations is the use of cast fiberglass components. They can be custom-tailored to the dimensions of the site. The fiberglass is strong, yet lightweight. It can be cut using small hand tools, and installation is easy. On the bottom row a series of marble columns replaced the original stone piers on this religious structure. A mold was made of the existing capital, They were cast in place at the base of each pier and could easily be raised to their position as capitals and secured in place with new steel angles.

201

COMMERCIAL RENOVATION

Many commercial establishments uncover old signage only to find elaborate ornamental detail hidden underneath. Such was the case in this renovation of an 1890s brick structure for a New York Barnes and Noble store, shown in the top row. In the middle row, drawings reveal items slated for restoration on this unique New York City structure. The bottom row shows the extent of work necessary to transform the Old Navy retail outlet into a modern store.

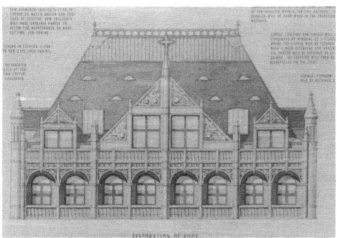
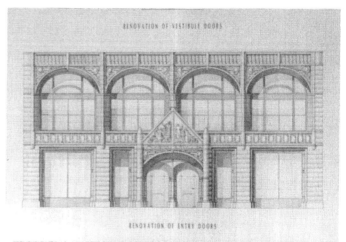

LARIMER SQUARE

This project was a pioneering one in many ways. It includes a block of nineteenth-century buildings adjacent to downtown Denver and an area scheduled for redevelopment. The old masonry walls of the buildings were reconstructed and left exposed instead of being hidden behind new materials, as was so often the case when this project was undertaken. Architectural details, cornices, and columns were restored by RNL as an integrated part of the restoration.

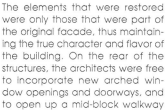

The elements that were restored were only those that were part of the original facade, thus maintaining the true character and flavor of the building. On the rear of the structures, the architects were free to incorporate new arched window openings and doorways, and to open up a mid-block walkway onto which shops and restaurants would open. Old and new are juxtaposed in complete harmony. To further add to the frontier atmosphere, a pair of carved animal heads was added at the impost position of an archway. One was the head of a bull, the other a head of a bear.

203

ERIE COMMUNITY COLLEGE

The renovation and adaptive reuse of a former federal building and post office in Buffalo, constructed in 1897, resulted in the creation of a city campus for a community college. Designed by Cannon, it contains educational and administrative functions, and is now a self-contained campus. The focal point of this Gothic structure is a large rectangular skylit atrium. The first floor was originally covered over, and was removed to open up the atrium to its full height.

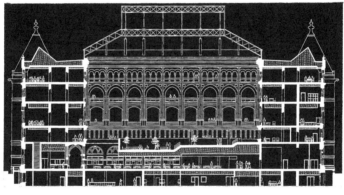

The exterior of the ornately detailed granite building has been restored. Unique features are the buffalo heads that appear at the spandrel base flanking the main entrance. The building is an example of Gothic style, characterized by pointed arches and a steep gable roof. The tower was reconstructed with new steel bracing and glazed, and the atrium skylight was replaced. The building was placed on the National Register of Historic Places in 1972. The rebirth of this abandoned landmark offers a living example on a major scale of the desirability and benefits of reuse.

ROCHESTER CITY HALL

A plaque in the lobby of the City Hall, which is undergoing restoration, outlines the history of the structure. In 1975 the Rochester City Council authorized the transfer of this former Federal Building, built in 1886, to the city for its preservation as a landmark and its rehabilitation for use by the community as a city hall. One of the features of the old building was its atrium court, which was engraved on the original plaque, along with a view of the exterior facade.

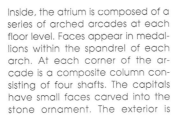

Inside, the atrium is composed of a series of arched arcades at each floor level. Faces appear in medallions within the spandrel of each arch. At each corner of the arcade is a composite column consisting of four shafts. The capitals have small faces carved into the stone ornament. The exterior is composed of rough stone with a series of corbels ringing the facade. Each corbel is supported by a carved stone face, which combines naturalistic features with vegetation and foliage. There are more than a dozen such faces, each with a different expression, yet all have similarities.

BLEECKER COURT

This project is notable not only for the design by Avinosh Malhotra but for the concept of salvage, restoration, and redevelopment by RockRose Construction. The project began with a burned-out shell of a building, with only the marble fa-cade standing. Located near New York's Greenwich Village, the living units were attractive to artists and students. The marble facade was first shored up from behind with steel bracing while a completely new structure was built behind it.

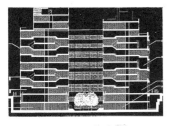

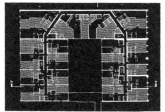

The main feature that tied the project together is the central courtyard, which is open to the sky, around which the new structures would be built. The use of the nine-teenth-century facade on one ex-posure, which produced high ceil-ings, combined with traditional floor-to-ceiling heights on the other exposures, resulted in mezzanines, sleeping lofts, and storage units for more usable square footage. It also provided for atypical apartment layouts. The restored facade fits within the historic fabric of the cast-iron district, while the opposite fa-cade shows a severely modern face to the nearby university.

MARSH AND MCLENNAN BUILDING

The adaptive use of one of Baltimore's last remaining cast-iron buildings by RTKL Associates integrates new construction with the restoration of an historic landmark. The resulting building provides office and commercial space and houses an area visitors' center. Constructed in 1871 as an office and warehouse, the original building is listed on the National Register of Historic Places, and exhibits a degree of ornamentation relatively rare in cast-iron structures.

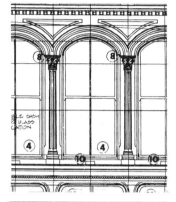

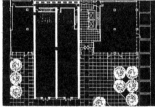

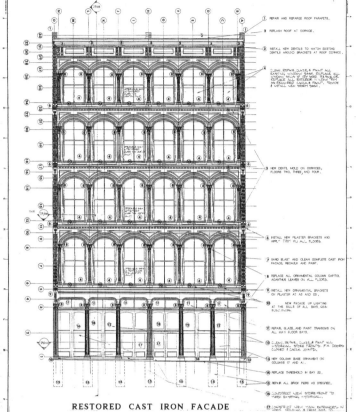

RESTORED CAST IRON FACADE

The architect's design goal was to create a unified statement without exaggerating either original or new building elements. The modern five-story addition extends and envelops the cast-iron building, retaining the scale and texture of both facades. A brise-soleil across the main facade echoes the texture of the cast-iron facade with thin extrusions dividing the clear glass into modules with the same proportions as the original building facade. The sloping wall or "ghost" of a three-story adjacent building is represented by granite panels on the blank facade, and hints at the original streetfront context.

207

CIRCLE CENTRE MALL

Large-scale complexes are not out of place in suburban malls, but are often overscaled for their urban neighborhoods. This project by the Centre Venture Architects in Indianapolis, solved the problem of relative scale by importing facades from other parts of the city to be re-erected on the site and joined with an existing facade that remained. Thus the superblock department store was almost unrecognizable except for the new entrances anchoring each end of the store.

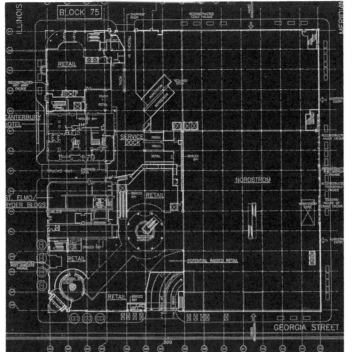

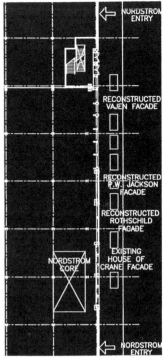

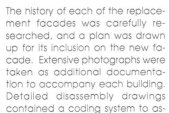

The history of each of the replacement facades was carefully researched, and a plan was drawn up for its inclusion on the new facade. Extensive photographs were taken as additional documentation to accompany each building. Detailed disassembly drawings contained a coding system to assist with the reconstruction of each facade on the new site. Each facade was then carefully dismantled and the remaining building demolished. The cast-iron pieces of one of the more distinguished facades were salvaged along with portions of the sheet metal cornice and stored in an open field.

Only two facades existed on the site of the new development. One of them was demolished after carefully removing the cast-iron storefront framing and limestone trim, which was stored in a warehouse. The facade left standing was used as the basis for duplicating many of the ornamental elements. All interior paneling and art glass were salvaged. Complete assembly drawings of the entire row of facades show the relationship of the newly assembled street facade. The photograph of the newly constructed facades show how they relate to the scale of the surrounding urban fabric.

The two Romanesque Revival-style buildings are in the only surviving row of Victorians in Manhattan; one housing a firehouse, designed in 1886 for horse-drawn vehicles, and the other a police station from the same year that was half the desired size for such a facility. The solution, by The Stein Partnership, was to join the services and put them behind the restored facades, adding space between them for their combined needs. A condition survey was done on the facades.

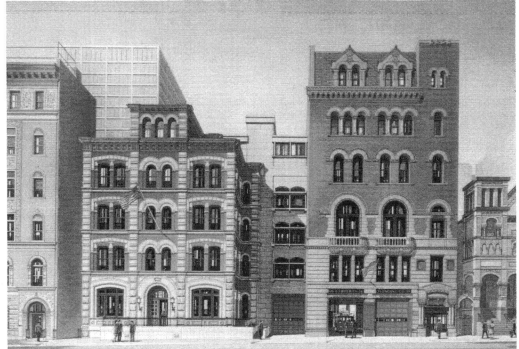

The police station facade was in good condition, but ornamentation and stonework were eroded on the firehouse. A specialist in ornamentation restoration took rubber molds directly from the building. Since there were no design or construction drawings to guide the work, the design team relied on photographs and descriptions in literature of the period and a style book that the original architect would have consulted. The goal was to preserve the flavor of the original stonecutter's style. Before demolishing the rear of both buildings, the facades were stabilized with heavy timber bracing.

Concern over the high cost and durability of stone replacements led the architect to choose cast stone. Plaster casts were made from the latex molds of the original stones. Missing ornament on the pilasters was recreated with modeling clay. A second latex mold was made and a plaster cast was reinforced with an armature before the cast stone mold was made. The molds can be used for as many as seven cast stone replacements. The completed ornamental blocks matched the original stones, and by replacing all the stones any differing weathering problems were eliminated.

SHEPARD HALL, CCNY

Few restoration projects better demonstrate the advantages of using computer technology in restoration work than the complex project shown here. It is the main building on an urban campus in New York City. The Stein Partnership was able to adopt a computerized process for documentation and development of contract documents and a data-base program to track every aspect of the work from shop drawings to the delivery of each component.

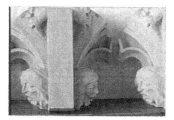

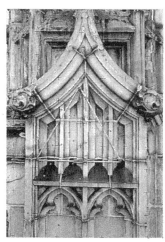

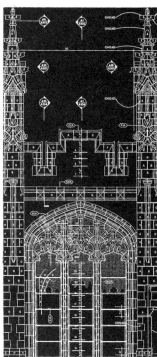

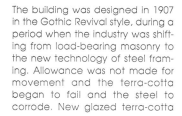

The building was designed in 1907 in the Gothic Revival style, during a period when the industry was shifting from load-bearing masonry to the new technology of steel framing. Allowance was not made for movement and the terra-cotta began to fail and the steel to corrode. New glazed terra-cotta was not used because it did not test satisfactorily. New materials included glass-fiber-reinforced compounds - concrete and polymers were used as they showed the greatest resistance to changes due to weather. This high-tech approach benefited not only the process but the final product.

BANANA REPUBLIC

This once elegant movie theater is located on a prominent corner in downtown Seattle. The theater was designed in 1918 by a local architect trained in Europe, who specialized in theater design. The original design's most impressive feature was a great glass dome and coffered vestibule at the corner. This was replaced in later years by an Art Deco design for the marquee that was totally out of character with the highly ornate and classical facade.

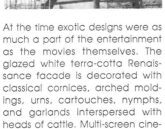

212

At the time exotic designs were as much a part of the entertainment as the movies themselves. The glazed white terra-cotta Renaissance facade is decorated with classical cornices, arched moldings, urns, cartouches, nymphs, and garlands interspersed with heads of cattle. Multi-screen cinemas in suburban malls reduced downtown movie audiences and brought many theaters to rubble. Renovating old theaters is not a new concept, as salvaging a historic building is usually not in conflict with sound retail decisions. This is particularly true of properties in prime downtown locations.

This classic old theater has recently been rejuvenated and adapted to Banana Republic's flagship store. In addition to cleaning and restoring the terra-cotta facade and restoring its storefronts, a large curved window area was added above the new entry. The most dramatic change to the facade occurred at the corner entrance. A projecting canopy was installed over the doorway reflecting the same design as the windows. This recalls the circular canopy of the original theater. Selective demolition ensured that ornamental elements were saved and incorporated into the interior spaces.

213

MELLON CENTER / MELLON INDEPENDENCE CENTER

Once an inspired gem in Pittsburgh's skyline, this eleven-story building lost much of its luster through years of neglect. The lush exterior consists of 1917 Flemish Gothic tracery and ornate dormer windows. It was designed originally as an office and arcade, and featured a ten-story, stained-glass-topped rotunda and a penthouse tower. All have been researched, restored, and brought up to contemporary office building standards by Burt Hill Kosar Rittlemann.

The Lit Bros. Building is a former century-old department store; it just barely ducked the wrecking ball. It was in shambles. The renovation and conversion to a modern office complex was done by Burt Hill Kosar Rittlemann. It consists of fifteen different structures constructed between 1859 and 1918.

The variety of facades reveals that the original owners chose to reuse existing buildings as they expanded, rather than tearing them down to house the department store as it grew. The exterior features a collection of cast-iron, brownstone and marble facades. The interior features a skylit atrium.

ST. REGIS HOTEL / ESSEX HOUSE NIKKO HOTEL

The St. Regis was built in 1901 as New York's most elegant skyscraper hotel. The exterior limestone facade needed cleaning and repointing, and exterior lighting was installed to highlight the intricacies of the windows, balconies and carved limestone. At the street level the original lobby was restored. Especially distinguished are the entrance revolving doors, the bronze doorman's sentry, which stands under the restored marquee, and the new street lamps.

The facade of this Art Deco exterior was cleaned, repointed, and restored. Custom-made windows increased views of New York's Central Park. A reclad bronze marquee and new signage recouped the style of the original design. By day the gilded ornament shines on the restored exterior. At night the ornament is highlighted by newly installed architectural lighting designed to enhance the ornamental detail. Both projects are by Brennan Beer Gorman Architects.

215

The Beaux-Arts-style building, listed on the National Register of Historic Places, was opened in Albany in 1900 as a station for the New York Central railroad. It featured an ornate plaster ceiling, two-story interior cast-iron facades created in an on-site foundry, and a granite facade. As the railroad era came to an end, so did Union Station. Vandals looted its architectural treasures, and weather destroyed its interior. The cast iron had rusted and the ornamental plaster worn away.

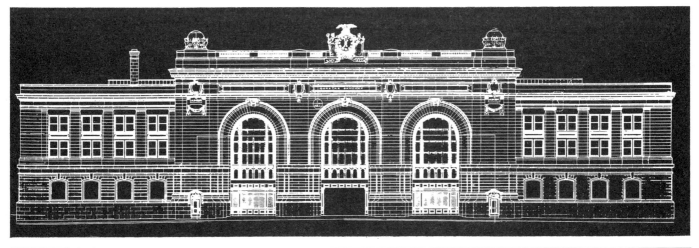

LOBBY SECTION - BEFORE

LOBBY SECTION - AFTER

The project was saved from demolition by a dedicated bank president, who transformed it into the bank's headquarters. Architects Einhorn Yaffee Prescott's solution not only increased the usable space twofold, but enhanced the drama and aesthetic quality of the original waiting room. The sectional views show that after restoration a second floor was added, the mezzanines were widened, and another mezzanine level was created. Many ceiling details were repeated in the cast-iron interior facade, which is composed of fluted columns, ornate railings and decorative ornament.

Other work on the cast-iron interior facade included replacing missing lion heads with plaster replicas, designing a new clock face based on photographs, and installing new windows and sashes. Eight-foot-high cartouches and keystone busts were cast in one piece. Rubber molds were made, and new plaster casts were painted and gilded according to the color scheme for the new ceiling. The large keystone is of Alexander the Great. Exterior work was not as extensive as that required on the interior, because it had been regularly maintained. The granite was gently cleaned and repaired.

MUSEUM CENTER AT UNION TERMINAL

This gracefully arched Art Deco masterpiece remained a popular symbol for the city long after train traffic halted in 1972. After twenty years and an unsuccessful attempt to rejuvenate the landmark as a retail center, the terminal is now the home for Cincinnati's Historical Society Museum and Natural History Museum. The focus of the renovation effort by Glaser Associates was to maintain the structure's historic and architectural integrity within the added new exhibits.

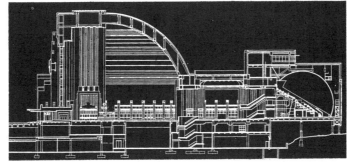

Attention to detail was given to the exterior restoration in preserving the delicate bas-relief sculptures that flank the main entrance. The Art Deco style of the station was preserved and enhanced throughout, and the rotunda area was carefully restored to recall the ambiance that greeted travelers at the former rail center. Because few color pictures were taken in the thirties, artisans had to rely on the recollections of conservators to duplicate the original paint shades on the domed rotunda ceiling. The skills of the restoration team gave this once obsolete landmark a new life as a model museum center.

The Orsay train station was on one of the most beautiful sites, across the Seine from the Louvre. It was constructed in 1900, and the ornamented facade contrasted with the metal and glass interior, a significant engineering feat. The abandoned train station was condemned but rescued from demolition in 1973. Five years later the plans for the museum were born. The building was placed on the Historic Building Inventory, and later classified as a National Monument.

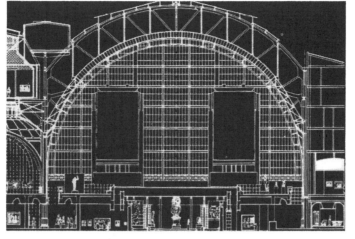

The restoration and transformation were awarded to winners of a competition, and the interior architecture was expertly adapted to the structure by architect Gae Aulenti, who conceived the new interior space as a new architecture adapted to an old structure. The result is a fine contemporary match. Many of the exhibits in the museum are replicas of architectural ornamentation and sculpture, including models and marble miniatures of architectural ornament on buildings throughout Paris. The sculpture, "Four Corners of the World," supports a celestial sphere in the main central gallery.

219

Older buildings that have outlived their usefulness are being transformed into economically viable structures by adapting them to a new purpose. The eighteen-year-old facade of this long-vacant San Francisco department store have been remodeled by Gensler and Associates as an office building for a major national bank. A pattern of light-colored glass and precast concrete panels replaced the windowless, original dark brick exterior facade with a bright one.

A fire gutted this ninety-seven-year-old national landmark in Denver, and began a race against time for renovating the historic structure. Only the two-foot-thick walls were left standing, so an entirely new structure was created by Gensler and Associates to support all interior walls. The new structure is secured to the old facade by 2500 two-foot-long bolts. The new structure reestablished the character of the original building. Previous alterations had blocked many of the windows which are now opened up again, and the street facade features new windows and a new arched entryway.

SHERATON MANHATTAN / INTERNATIONAL PLACE

Once considered a "motor inn," this New York hotel underwent a significant visual transformation of the facade. It is now a first-class business hotel with a reconfigured lobby. The exterior was reclad with bays of reflective glass and panels of acrylic cement. All the masonry was repaired. New decorative metal grillwork camouflages the parking garage at the hotel's base. The lower facade also received new lighting and new storefronts by architects Brennan Beer Gorman.

A building can be old enough to look dated but not old enough to be considered a classic. This aging twelve-story mixed-use structure fit that category, yet its prime location was justification to consider renovating it. Architects Brennan Beer Gorman determined that the dated sixties curtainwall had to go.

The design team likened the reconstruction challenge to rebuilding a human body which had been stripped down to a skeleton. A new module was established for the new facade skin, based on current trends in office design, and a stronger base was added to give the building a new look.

Donald Trump and Philip Johnson paired up to create this International Hotel and Tower. This new building uses the steel skeleton of an older structure, and wraps it with angled columns and spandrels of gold reflective glass; the columns are tipped with stainless steel strips. This method of turning worn-out structures into new ones is a specialty of Trump, who began his development career by turning a solid, load-bearing structure into a glittering glass facade.

Many of the classic highrises of the 1960s need new facades, as the curtainwall structures reach the end of their cycle. They do not make very good ruins. Architects Swanke Hayden Connell found that a new skin was the answer. The 1962 curtainwall was removed, the steel frame was reinforced and expanded, and the entire tower was reclad in granite and aluminum panels by Turner Construction Company. Stainless-steel decorative members articulate the facade. Stainless steel finials cap each horizontal level as they step progressively upwards towards the new ornamental tower.

CHICAGO HISTORICAL SOCIETY

When the plans for renovation of this 1931 Georgian Revival brick building and austere 1972 white marble addition were formulated, the goal was to increase storage space and improve staff facilities. The addition had a cold, mausoleum-like appearance so that nobody liked to visit. It soon became clear that a new addition would accomplish a more important objective: improving the Society's image by making the building more visually appealing.

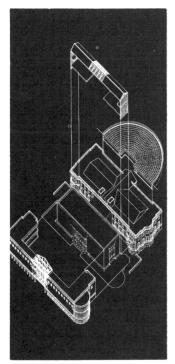

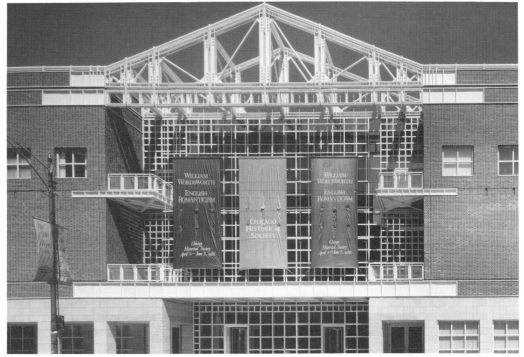

The axonometric on the left shows how the new addition wraps around and encases the 1972 addition and joins it with the original brick structure. The new addition by architects Holabird and Root, increases its dimensions on three sides and provides much needed space, as well as a more welcoming image. The new addition harmonizes in scale and materials with the 1931 building, with white steel and structural glass wall giving a modern expression to the traditional brick and limestone. A white steel truss and glass wall grid hung with colorful banners create a dramatic entrance.

PALACE OF FINE ARTS

The history of this structure is perhaps one of the most unusual in the annals of preservation. It was not built once, but twice: the first time as a temporary part of an international exposition; the second time as a permanent part of the city. In 1906 San Francisco had been reduced to rubble by an earthquake, but fought back to not only rebuild the city, but take on the 1915 Pan-Pacific International Exposition, celebrating the opening of the Panama Canal.

The building represents one of the most sensitive expressions of an architectural concept in modern times. Bernard Maybeck wanted the building to represent beauty modified by sadness, and chose an old Roman ruin as his theme. Virtually every form of ornamentation heightened this effect. A lagoon made the vast rotunda appear as if on an island, overgrown with trees. When the exposition closed and other buildings were razed, the palace remained. The temporary nature of the structure gradually weathered to a genuine ruin. Civic efforts and private donations brought it back to life.

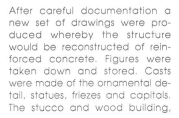

After careful documentation a new set of drawings were produced whereby the structure would be reconstructed of reinforced concrete. Figures were taken down and stored. Casts were made of the ornamental detail, statues, friezes and capitals. The stucco and wood building, which had stood as a temporary structure for 45 years, was torn down and completely reconstructed. This kind of effort has never been seen before, but is a prime example of the importance of keeping our architectural heritage, particularly when it involves buildings as noteworthy as this one.

ELLIS ISLAND NATIONAL MUSEUM OF IMMIGRATION

Closed as an immigration station in 1945, Ellis Island lay abandoned for nearly thirty years. The effects of this neglect were devastating: salt water seeped through masonry; roofs rotted letting in rain and snow; and plaster fell from the walls, filling some rooms waist-high with debris. In 1982, the National Park Service decided to fully restore the main building and powerhouse. The main building, one of the largest restoration projects undertaken in the country, was opened in 1990.

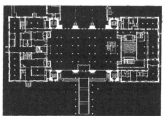

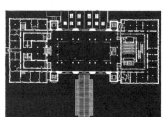

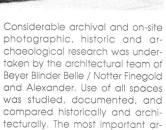

Considerable archival and on-site photographic, historic and archaeological research was undertaken by the architectural team of Beyer Blinder Belle / Notter Finegold and Alexander. Use of all spaces was studied, documented, and compared historically and architecturally. The most important areas were faithfully restored to the original, while other spaces were converted to modern needs. The design team realized that their problem was the same as for its original use: that of accommodating large numbers of people arriving at the island by boat twelve months a year.

Some of the building's most important architectural elements had been removed during earlier remodelings, and the team designed replacements that would fit into the restored spaces but would not be perceived by visitors as pieces of the building's original fabric. The paved promenade, covered by a glass steel canopy, connects the ferry pier to the main entrance. The design is an interpretation of the original, demolished in 1930, but built of contemporary glass and steel. The exterior stone and brick were cleaned and repaired, including the large keystone heads over the arched windows.

STATUE OF LIBERTY

Most Americans have grown very accustomed to the image of the Statue of Liberty, standing in New York Harbor for over a century. No one can doubt that the originator, sculptor Federic Auguste Bartholdi, understood the technical demands of monumental art very well. Starting with a small terracotta statue, he increased the size through three larger scaled versions, finally erecting the statue in Paris, where it was disassembled and shipped to New York.

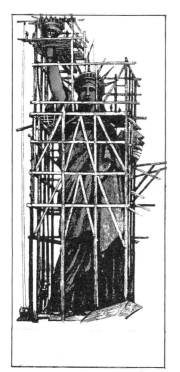

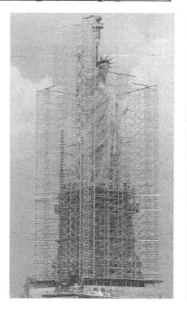

The sculptor had the forethought to commission French engineer Alexander Gustave Eiffel to design internal support for the 151-foot statue. He devised an iron skeleton to support the copper skin that holds the drapery's folds. After a century of standing in the elements, the statue began to show its age. A team of advisors was formed with consulting architects Swanke Hayden Connell. The illustration above shows the scaffolding constructed in France and the bracing of the famous face. Modern models built by the architects from measured drawings were assisted with computer technology.

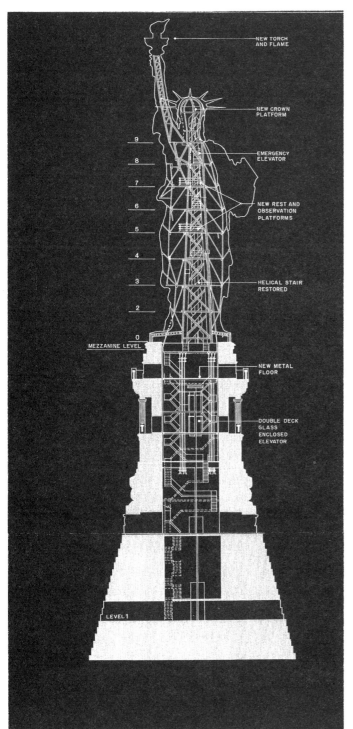

NEW TORCH AND FLAME

NEW CROWN PLATFORM

EMERGENCY ELEVATOR

NEW REST AND OBSERVATION PLATFORMS

HELICAL STAIR RESTORED

9
8
7
6
5
4
3
2
0

MEZZANINE LEVEL

NEW METAL FLOOR

DOUBLE DECK GLASS ENCLOSED ELEVATOR

LEVEL 1

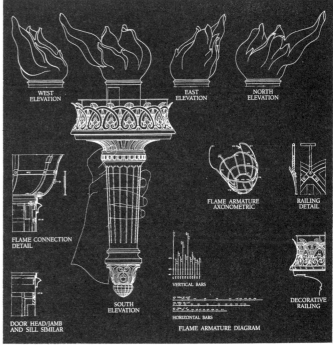

WEST ELEVATION

EAST ELEVATION

NORTH ELEVATION

FLAME CONNECTION DETAIL

FLAME ARMATURE AXONOMETRIC

RAILING DETAIL

DOOR HEAD/JAMB AND SILL SIMILAR

SOUTH ELEVATION

VERTICAL BARS

HORIZONTAL BARS

FLAME ARMATURE DIAGRAM

DECORATIVE RAILING

Liberty's torch carries a heavy symbolic load, second only to the statues location as the gateway to the New World. The flame has always been the weakest link in the statue's integrity. The original design by Bartholdi was a copper flame covered with gold leaf. Many modifications were made, most of which failed. The restoration team restored the original gilded finish. All the fabrication for the restoration took place in workshops open to the public, just as Bartholdi's was open a hundred years ago. A full-size copper model of Liberty's face is visible in the museum at the base of the statue.

R E N E W A L

After two hundred years we are finally beginning to place some value on our architectural heritage. We are awakening to the fact that we have been destroying the very fabric of our cities and the architectural details that we now consider very important. Many Americans travel to Europe and elsewhere to enjoy an ambience that comes from being among relics of the past, but few relate this experience to our own country. We can clearly see how desolate Rome or Venice might be if those structures had been replaced with modern highrises. Florence and Paris would look just like New York or Chicago. (In fact, the new Paris does, but it is located in a separate city, far from the monuments and traditional architecture.)

The building restoration movement has been one important factor in rekindling our interest in architectural detail and ornament. The preservation movement has accomplished in the United States what the Modern Movement claimed to be trying to accomplish, but never did. They wanted to establish a vision of new possibilities, but were too limited in their methodology and use of forms. Preservation and restoration have forced us to respond to a new vision, because architects have been forced to confront ornament once again. They need to study architectural ornament, because it was omitted from their Modernist education. They have to learn how it works, how to encompass it into adaptive reuse projects, and even how to design it anew.

Restoration has also forced us to focus our attention on crafts that had almost disappeared. They were simply in hibernation and are being re-assimilated into architecture, not just as afterthoughts but as an integral part of the design process. This heightened appreciation for richness in detail is evidenced by the fact that we want more than plain white walls. We want color and visual intrigue. Ever since 1966, when architect Robert Venturi claimed that "less is a bore," the attitude toward ornamental detail has dramatically changed. His thoughts were shared by a small group of architects, among them Charles Moore, then chair of the Yale School of Architecture. His design for the Piazza d'Italia, with its Doric, Ionic, and Corinthian columns, pilastered arcade and grand arches, is an evocation of a nineteenth-century Neoclassical building rather than actually being one. Major public spaces are being designed almost as stage sets, evoking historical devices that are references to the past, but with a fresh contemporary look.

A significant development has been the incorporation of existing facades into new projects which are generally of much grander scale. They add a much needed element of personal scale at the street level, and enrich new buildings with period ornamental details. Another significant factor that we learned from preservation involves the use of ornamental details that are incorporated into contemporary structures, both as a historic commemorative act and as one that is visually appealing. Many new facades creatively capture the essence of classical elements and incorporate them in a contemporary mix.

The renewed use of architectural ornament, whether it is reclaimed from past structures or designed anew, is a sign that the creative force is still alive in architecture. It promises a future that will look much different from what we have known for the better part of this century.

233

There is a growing practice of conserving and salvaging portions of buildings that once existed on the sites of redeveloped urban areas, whether for new structures or open plazas. This is certainly better than losing the richness of the ornamental detail altogether, and it obviously enhances the new structure. The top row shows a fountain structure in an open plaza in Seattle. The terra-cotta pilasters from the demolished building are incorporated into the new structure.

The middle row shows an open plaza fronting a high-rise structure in Seattle. Ornamentation from the building it replaced is worked into a lower structure at its base. The right image shows an ornamental frieze that was salvaged from the razed structure and incorporated into a parapet on the plaza level of the new structure. The bottom row features a pavillion constructed over the entry to an underground cafe. The arches previously appeared on the facade of the building that stood at that location. The ornamental arches features a frieze of horned faces above a ram's head keystone.

RECYCLED STREET FACADES

Many small-scale commercial structures in urban areas have been demolished to make room for larger structures. What the new structures lack is a convincing human scale, which is precisely what is found in the original structures!

Salvaging the ornamental elements not only makes sense from a conservationist's point of view, but these elements can be integrated into the new facade to provide an aesthetic appeal. This is exemplified here in a variety of projects.

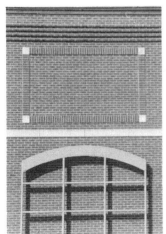

The top panels show how salvaged architectural ornaments were incorporated into a completely modern commercial streetscape in Vancouver. The new design relates to the existing ornament through the use of articulated joints in the new facade. The middle panels show a minimalist approach to preserving a facade as a ghostly screen for a parking lot in Portland. The facade shell is supported by steel braces. The bottom row shows how the shell of an old building is preserved as a screen behind which new commercial space was created in the redeveloped old market section of Omaha.

COMMEMORATIVE ORNAMENT

In the late 1800s hotels were springing up all over Seattle, and the Savoy was the queen. Today it is replaced with a high-rise structure, which carries a plaque reading: "You are standing on a block whose history reflects an important chapter into the past. A glimpse of the elegance of the Savoy Hotel is afforded by the castings adjacent to this plaque. These castings capture the beauty of the decorative relief sculptures that topped the capitals inside the hotel."

On the street level of a new Seattle high-rise, a plaque described the history of the previous building. The bronze castings set into the stone were executed by a local artist. They are exact replicas of original castings taken from the predecessor and carry northwestern motifs. The bottom row shows the roof structure of a new skyscraper in Vancouver, which replaced a medical facility. Although severely modern, the new structure copied details from the old building, incorporated them into spandrel designs, and reused sculptured figures on the new parapets and ornamented areas of a courtyard.

MISSOURI COURT OF APPEALS

This small-scale brick building in Kansas City, by Abend Singleton Associates, is adjacent to many other monumental limestone-clad buildings in the government center located one block away. The main axis of the building is placed on a diagonal relationship with the ceremonial axis pointing to the government center. A major limestone portal frames the building's entrance to enlarge the scale and create a symbolic reference to other government buildings.

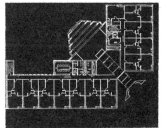

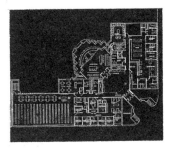

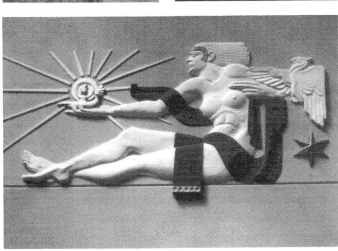

The court building houses a courtroom and chambers with adjoining administrative areas, offices, conference rooms, law library and research area. The public lobby and entrance to the Appeals Court are framed by the bas-relief sculptures of "Lex," Latin for law, and "Pax," Latin for peace. The figure "Lex," holding the radiating golden icon and an eagle on her shoulder, symbolizes the judicial system's search for meaning in society. These bas-relief sculptures were derived from similar motifs in the original building, where the court was housed for many years until moving to this new facility.

237

BIOSPHERE 2: TONY PRICE SCULPTURES

Biosphere 2 is a high-tech pyramidal structure in the Arizona mountains designed as an ecological system to recycle air, water, wastes and nutrients and to support plant and animal species as well as human habitation. On the grounds of Biosphere 2 and on one of its many ancillary facilities are the sculptures of artist Tony Price. Some of Price's most imposing pieces include bells built out of hydrogen-bomb casings and life-size sculptures built out of recycled rocket parts.

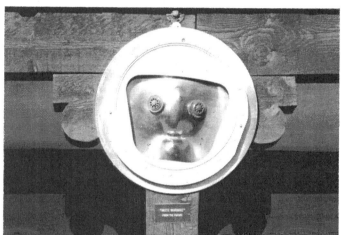

He started making these unique pieces after a trip to the Los Alamos National Labratory, home of the first nuclear weapons. He became attracted to the machined precision of the scrapped metallic pieces, and began fashioning sculptures and masks that echo religious and peaceful themes. A series of faces that appears on the posts surrounding the gift shop and post office is serious, curious, humorous and most of all visually appealing.

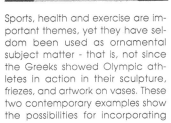

Sports, health and exercise are important themes, yet they have seldom been used as ornamental subject matter - that is, not since the Greeks showed Olympic athletes in action in their sculpture, friezes, and artwork on vases. These two contemporary examples show the possibilities for incorporating physical activities into architectural ornamental panels. The top image is the Nike store in Chicago, where cast aluminum figures in panels appear to be emerging from the building's facade. The lower panels show a sports outlet in New York City, where the figures appear on pilasters at the street level.

239

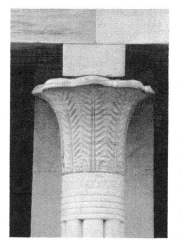

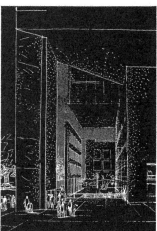

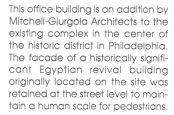

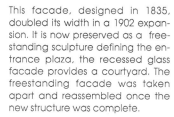

240

This office building is an addition by Mitchell-Giurgola Architects to the existing complex in the center of the historic district in Philadelphia. The facade of a historically significant Egyptian revival building originally located on the site was retained at the street level to maintain a human scale for pedestrians.

This facade, designed in 1835, doubled its width in a 1902 expansion. It is now preserved as a freestanding sculpture defining the entrance plaza, the recessed glass facade provides a courtyard. The freestanding facade was taken apart and reassembled once the new structure was complete.

FRANKLIN COURT / PIAZZA d'ITALIA

Sometimes it is impossible to reconstruct an old facade for lack of sufficient historic data. Architects, Venturi, Rausch and Scott Brown chose to memorialize Benjamin Franklin on the site of his home and print shop in Philadelphia in a unique way; by creating a "ghost" framework of steel to recall the lost buildings. The remains of the old foundation are viewed through glass canopies. Below is a large museum and theater. Other restored structures hold additional exhibits.

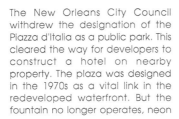

The New Orleans City Council withdrew the designation of the Piazza d'Italia as a public park. This cleared the way for developers to construct a hotel on nearby property. The plaza was designed in the 1970s as a vital link in the redeveloped waterfront. But the fountain no longer operates, neon tubes are broken, marble and tile are cracked, and the brilliant Post-modern color scheme faded. It is now an unused magnificent ruin. The original arched fountain, sporting a pair of cartouches of its architect, Charles Moore, has dried up. The plaza is now a ghost and in desparate need of rejuvenation.

One of the most important elements of a facade is the entrance. It is the main focal point and the area which most people see in passing by and use in entering the structure. Throughout history the entry has received special treatment by the use of figures or other architectural forms. This branch of the Public Library in Toronto has incorporated many elements into the facade that highlight and emphasize the entrance, including the use of figures.

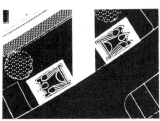

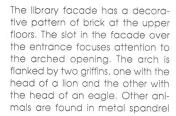

The library facade has a decorative pattern of brick at the upper floors. The slot in the facade over the entrance focuses attention to the arched opening. The arch is flanked by two griffins, one with the head of a lion and the other with the head of an eagle. Other animals are found in metal spandrel panels, and the cast image of an owl is set into the brick wall at the street level. The bottom panels show the entry pylons of the Best Products headquarters, where the entry is marked by two pylons with stone eagles which were salvaged from an abandoned airline terminal building in New York City.

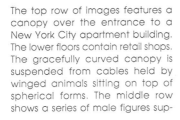

The top row of images features a canopy over the entrance to a New York City apartment building. The lower floors contain retail shops. The gracefully curved canopy is suspended from cables held by winged animals sitting on top of spherical forms. The middle row shows a series of male figures supporting a canopy with an undulating front edge. This hotel is being renovated in Miami Beach's Art Deco district. The bottom row shows a contemporary canopy in front of a vintage retail shop. Small faces inside each pilaster capital perhaps represent important local personages.

243

TROMPE L'OEIL

The phrase "trompe l'oeil" means that which fools the eye. Painting architectural scenes on blank spaces is as old as the ceiling panels of Egypt or wall murals of Pompeii. Recently, artists have rediscovered the power of murals, once confined to interior spaces, and have applied them to the blank facades of buildings. The blank wall of a Boston apartment faces an open corner lot. The ground-to-roof mural depicts the facade of a period cafe.

244

On the middle left, architectural details are continued in paint on the side of a New York facade. The windows are real. The Venetian facade, complete with gondolas, is on a long blank wall fronting a parking lot in Minneapolis. The bottom murals are by artist Richard Haas. The left image is of pioneers in Portland. The middle mural is the painted arched vista to the Fontainbleau, which was blocked by a blank wall. The arched monumental entry is on a building in Cincinnati. The seven- story mural was inspired by Piranesi's study for reconstruction of the temple of Vesta, and is called "Cincinnatus."

In this project Ricnard Haas associated with architect George C. T. Woo to remedy an aesthetic problem with a building built in 1958. It was sheathed with aluminum fins and clashed with the 1895 Renaissance Revival court house next door. More than paint was involved. The mural was applied over a curtainwall structure of synthetic stucco designed by the architect. The original 1958 design was decorated with four monumental Art Moderne angels in bas relief. These were retained in the mural but now hover under tall Roman arches, and relate to the neighboring court house.

245

Creative facades characterize this group of architects who use each program as raw material from which to create art. The top project is the Molino Stucky site in Venice. The promenade deck is substituted by a series of nine re- constructions on graduated levels, progressively engulfed by the lagoon. The inversion of the relationship between the canals of Venice and the building facade makes the facade the horizontal element, the wall of water the facade.

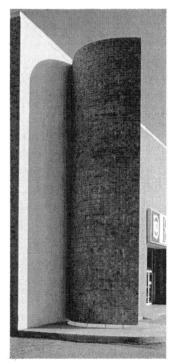

The middle row shows the Forest Building, which gives the appearance of architecture invaded by nature. The two images of the Notch Showroom show the main entryway with a raw-edged gap removed from one corner. When closed only a single fissure is visible. The Tilt Showroom is an inversion of architectural equilibrium, in which the facade tilts precariously on one edge. The Cutler Ridge Showroom's facade is fragmented and segmented into four successive reductions which together make up the whole facade, The Peel Showroom facade was curved at the edge, exposing the undersurface.

For the Frankfurt Museum of Modern Art project at the top, SITE decided to place a rectangular building on a triangular site. To do this required bisecting the volume with a pie-shaped space frame, thus exposing the interior through a rough cutaway rather than in a formalistic manner. It created a more dramatic dialogue between the interior and exterior facade. In the Inside/Outside building large sections of the exterior facade have been broken away to reveal the interior. The exterior was treated with merchandise, which was "ghosted" through the use of monochrome gray paint.

JAMES WHITCOMB RILEY HOSPITAL FOR CHILDREN

This hospital's original 1924 facility and 1971 addition at Indiana University were renovated and expanded using a variety of human-interest themes by Ellerbe Associates. The cascading roof lines and facade setbacks echo the scale of the original Georgian buildings. The exterior court is an abstraction of a house, and the glass-roofed atrium lobby connects the new addition to the earlier buildings. Fanciful statuary is used as a common thread throughout the complex.

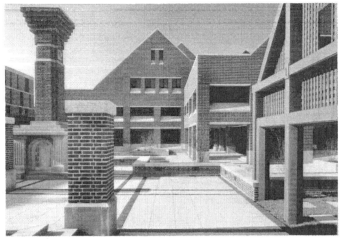 

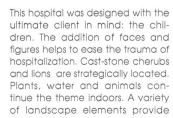

This hospital was designed with the ultimate client in mind: the children. The addition of faces and figures helps to ease the trauma of hospitalization. Cast-stone cherubs and lions are strategically located. Plants, water and animals continue the theme indoors. A variety of landscape elements provide experiences for patients and visitors alike, such as the fountain parapet featuring the cherub faces. The new addition joins with two earlier buildings by doming a former outdoor space to make a new lobby. The brick facade of the original Georgian-style building is a striking contrast to the new addition.

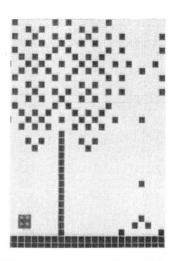

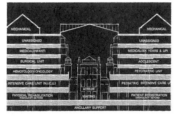

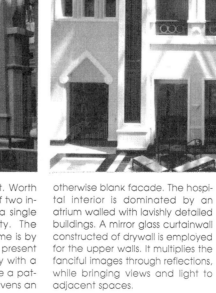

This children's hospital in Ft. Worth resulted from the merger of two independent hospitals into a single new replacement facility. The exterior architectural scheme is by David M. Schwartz At the present time bridges link the facility with a neighboring hospital, where a pattern of mosaic tile trees enlivens an otherwise blank facade. The hospital interior is dominated by an atrium walled with lavishly detailed buildings. A mirror glass curtainwall constructed of drywall is employed for the upper walls. It multiplies the fanciful images through reflections, while bringing views and light to adjacent spaces.

This Chicago building occupies a full city block bounded by major streets and historic buildings. It recalls other civic buildings in its design, as sculptural ornament and the large scale of architectural detail establish a degree of granduer.

The classical language was chosen by architects Hammond Beeby and Babka, to reflect a slice of time from Greece to the present time, and classicism provided the richest vocabulary of conventionalized ornament for its facade.

250

The entire building is conceived in the outline of an immense Greek temple. The columns are replaced with a rhythmic collonnade of vertical pendants suspended from giant festoons immediately below a bracketed ornamental railing. The pediments at the corner of the roof contain metal sculptures representing the antefix and acroterion silhouetted by immense feathered palmettes, representing life. Guarding the four corners are large owls, symbolic of wisdom. An owl prepares for flight above the main entrance while grasping a book. These large creatures are fashioned out of metal.

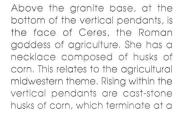

Above the granite base, at the bottom of the vertical pendants, is the face of Ceres, the Roman goddess of agriculture. She has a necklace composed of husks of corn. This relates to the agricultural midwestern theme. Rising within the vertical pendants are cast-stone husks of corn, which terminate at a roundel encasing the head of a cherub blowing air. Draped between the roundels are giant festoons of white oak leaves, representing the official Chicago tree. Within the leaves is an abundance of fruit and vegatables similar to a medallion on the old Chicago Public Library.

SEATTLE ART MUSEUM

The sloping site contributed much to the design of this museum, and many of the building's functions are expressed at the street level in the unusual facade designed by Robert Venturi and Denise Scott Brown. The curved facade at the lower end opens the street corner, with giant 14-foot-high letters that spell out the name of the building incised in the wall above. The slope of the hill is exposed in two terraced parallel stairs, one indoors and one at the sidewalk.

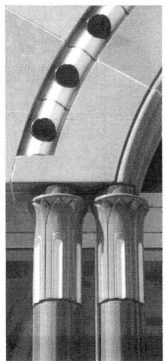

At the sidewalk level, the facade is festooned with colorful pilasters and a playful band of pink granite arches running over triangular and arched pediments to a dramatic entrance at the upper corner. The fanciful Moorish arches are accompanied by multicolored terracotta tile panels. The upper facade by contrast is a solid mass, articulated by the incised letters and an irregular modular grid pattern in the concrete panels. The use of unabashed decorative elements and the contrast in colors give the building scale at the pedestrian level and become a work of art in themselves.

The "Team Disney" building was designed by Arata Isozaki as the administrative heart of Walt Disney World Resort; it showcases the style of "entertainment architecture." Two four-story wings are joined by a 120-foot tower, which has a giant cylindrical sundial on the interior wall. A variety of geometric shapes in primary colors dominate the facade. Twenty-foot circles form Mickey Mouse ears at the main entry, which are repeated in two entrance gateways to the site.

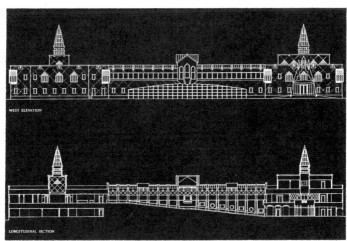

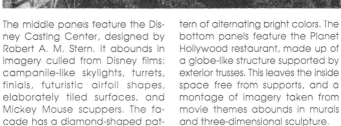

The middle panels feature the Disney Casting Center, designed by Robert A. M. Stern. It abounds in imagery culled from Disney films: campanile-like skylights, turrets, finials, futuristic airfoil shapes, elaborately tiled surfaces, and Mickey Mouse scuppers. The facade has a diamond-shaped pattern of alternating bright colors. The bottom panels feature the Planet Hollywood restaurant, made up of a globe-like structure supported by exterior trusses. This leaves the inside space free from supports, and a montage of imagery taken from movie themes abounds in murals and three-dimensional sculpture.

253

THEME FACADES

Today, the use of themes in designing structures is widespread. Perhaps this is the result of theme parks and other forms of entertainment architecture. It shows a desire to identify the building with a concept rather than relying on classical or traditional motifs for the facade. The top row of images show the facade of New York's Jeckyl and Hyde Restaurant. It has an eclectic style that combines classical motifs with other macabre forms of ornamentation.

In Atlantic City, a Ripley's Museum opened to the surprise of people strolling the boardwalk. The facade is apparently split by the accidental breaking of a chain that held a wrecking ball, which is in the shape of a globe. The ball crashed through the facade, splitting it in pieces, as surprised workers look on from the top. The facade issues steam at sporadic intervals. The Ripley's in Orlando has a normal interior floor level, but the exterior looks like it is sinking into the ground on one end. The happy figure on the left is offset by the one on the right who is struggling to keep the facade from falling.

MAYFAIR IN THE GROVE / MAYFAIR HOUSE

Mayfair In The Grove, a tropical shopping center, is an integration of all its functions; boutiques, cafes, art and crafts, and as a place in the overall environment of the village of Coconut Grove. Architect Kenneth Treister designed the project to express an integration of art, architecture and the relation to the community. The village is a lushly landscaped street-scape of small shops and restaurants, and this character is reflected in the "anti-mall" environment of Mayfair.

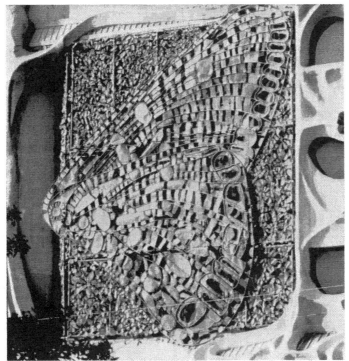

A hotel was later added to the existing Mayfair shopping complex. Its three story facade over two levels of shops consists of wood trellised openings, covered with flowering vines. On the corner, a large sculptured copper butterfly filters light for the corner suites. The design exemplifies the artistic collaboration of the craftspeople and the items designed by the architect which includes ceramics, stained glass, sculpture, fresco paintings, bas-relief and interior furnishings. Three floors of suites surround open atriums, landscaped with lush fern and a water garden that covers the entire ground level.

LOUVRE PYRAMID

The museum building of the Louvre never fully functioned for the presentation and storage of its vast treasures. In 1981 the Ministry of Finance, which had offices inside the Louvre, was relocated, and the Grand Louvre project was born.

The existing buildings were completely remodeled. Walls were removed, floors taken out. Important architectural landmarks were preserved in all their original splendor. As the sole occupant the museum became a modern facility.

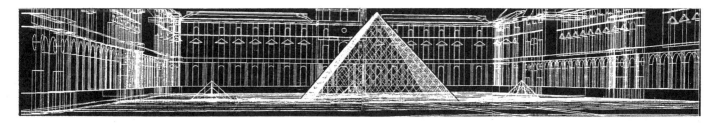

The architectural symbol of the pyramid, designed by I. M. Pei, expresses simplicity and solidarity. The structure of the new pyramid, a very fine mesh of stainless steel tubes and cables, allows sunlight into the hall below. The view from inside the new concourse up through the net of steel and glass frames the encrusted classical facades of the old building beyond. Since the Palace had been remodeled over and over during the past three centuries, reflecting all the popular architectural styles of the day, the new museum would once again reflect the architecture of our time.

ARAB WORLD INSTITUTE

Situated in the center of Paris, this building was designed by Jean Nouvel, Pierre Soria, Gilbert Lezenes and Architecture-Studio as a series of transparent facades. They all respond individually to the major site factors. The northern facade is a traditional glass and grid plane. The curved glass wall reflects images from the opposite banks of the Seine and responds to the curved street fronting the river. The curtain-wall grid suggests the courses of a traditional stone wall.

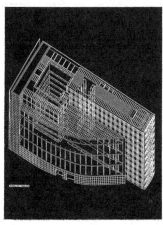

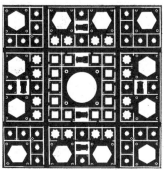

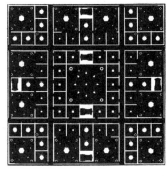

257

The southern facade combines 27,000 diaphrams in 252 panels to produce a high-tech sun screen of Arabic origin. The entire facade was designed to respond to a light sensor which controls the tiny diaphragms within the panels, similar to the shutter of a camera lens. Each of the facades is well delineated both in plan and elevation, and each expresses a different function. They all have mechanistic metaphors, analogies, images and different expressions, yet they retain a high-tech harmony among them. It is one of the few buildings in the world that is "alive" in responding to its environment.

The Pompidou Center in Paris, designed by Richard Rogers and Renzo Piano, winners of an international competition, takes functionalism to the extreme. Early modernists were content just to express a building's structure in the exterior facade. Here the entire functional components of the structure; elevators, escalators, pipes for water and ducts for air conditioning, were exposed on the exterior of the facade. The design of the facades is intentionally "inside out": a high-tech structural system of columns, struts, cables, and fasteners provides the visual stimulation that fenestration and ornament usually provide. Exterior escalators add a diagonal element running across the facade, with access levels occurring at each floor and terminating at the top of the structure. This unusual design has sparked more controversy than any other building in modern times. One theory relates the "scaffolding" look to the many historic buildings in Paris that are constantly undergoing restoration, and this motif is carried out on the facade as a permanent scaffold. The result is that the cultural center and library have become one of the most popular attractions in Paris.

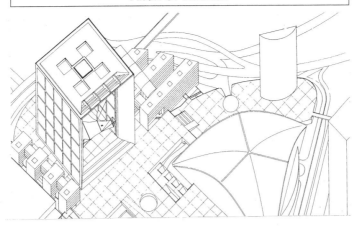

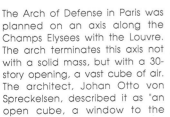

The Arch of Defense in Paris was planned on an axis along the Champs Elysees with the Louvre. The arch terminates this axis not with a solid mass, but with a 30-story opening, a vast cube of air. The architect, Johan Otto von Spreckelsen, described it as "an open cube, a window to the world." The arch is a cube of smooth glass panels and white marble contrasted by a delicate counterpoint. Stretched within the opening of the cube are cable and fabric tensile forms that float like clouds in the space. The delicate vertical steel and cable structure that supports the glass eleva-tor provides another element of counterpoint. The exterior facades of the cube have a bright surface symbolizing a microchip, the most brilliant invention of modern com-munication. The facade walls in-side the cube have a gridlike fen-estration covering the entire sur-face. On the far side of the plat-form are overlapping vertical sheets of glass, forming a barrier from the wind and diminishing traf-fic noise without interrupting the vista. The building is totally unique and avoids the usual modern cliches in place of a modern mon-umentality.

259

YOHGA BUILDING PROJECT / LIBRARY SQUARE

The concept for this project in Tokyo, designed by The Callison Partnership, produced a highly visible building that would accommodate a large advertising billboard oriented towards an adjacent expressway. The building's fa-cades that faces the expressway features a curved stone wall that is a small-scale reproduction of a section of the Coliseum in Rome. The opposite side features two straight walls of glass that reflect the rectilinear grid of the city.

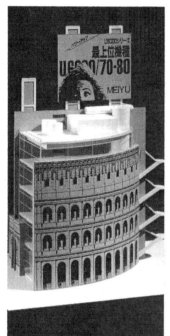

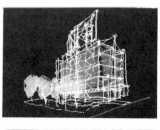

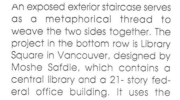

An exposed exterior staircase serves as a metaphorical thread to weave the two sides together. The project in the bottom row is Library Square in Vancouver, designed by Moshe Safdie, which contains a central library and a 21- story federal office building. It uses the colonnade to evoke the classical language of traditional library architecture. Further, it evokes images of the coliseum in Rome with its open-ended colonnade. Bridges span the skylit interiors between the two oval-shaped forms.

E Walk *sm* on the New 42nd Street

The legendary mecca of good times is getting a major hotel in addition to the many theater renovations already completed in the area. It is a soaring tourist and meeting hotel, designed by Arquitectonica, rising above an entertainment / retail complex designed by D'Agostino Izzo Quirk. The developer and builder is Tishman Urban Development Corporation, a unit of Tishman Realty & Construction Company, with vast entertainment-hotel experience.

This bold design embodies all the fantasies of this legendary crossroads, and will feature these elements in its facades. Its design is a vertical triptych. At the base it will retain the existing scale of the neighboring low-rise buildings with restaurants, shops, and theaters. A 10-story boutique hotel will rise above one corner, and the 45-story glass tower will rise above it with the flash of a meteor. A curving streak of light from the tower's base to the top represents the meteor's tail. Immense signs will appear on the retail area in a neon pop-art parade, while a tower will display continuous video images.

The dolphin and swan symbols were chosen as the aquatic theme for these hotels, as they both front on a lagoon. They are consistent with the character of the surrounding Disney development at Epcot Center, called "entertainment architecture." The facade of the triangular tower of the Dolphin looks much like a pyramid in frontal view and is the dominant feature of the complex. Each of the four wings of the Dolphin is topped with a monumental 25-foot urn and a 60-foot-high dolphin at each end of the building. In the center of the facade, water cascades down several tiers into clamshell fountains, and ends in a clamshell pool supported by four dolphin-shaped supports. The patterns on the lower portion of the Dolphin resemble banana leaves, while on the Swan they resemble waves. The color scheme for both hotels is blue-green and coral. The Swan is topped by five-story swan sculptures. The larger-than-life figures were constructed on a metal and wood frame with multiple layers of fiberglass as the final form. The original sketch by the architect was first sculpted out of styrofoam by a Disney artist. The image was transferred to a digital database for creating the full size forms.

Luxor Las Vegas is a 30-story pyramid encased in 11 acres of dark reflective glass. The hotel's Egyptian theme reflects the grandeur of the 4300-year-old predecessor through out. The hotel is identified by a giant obelisk. Guests arrive by way of an avenue of reclining sphinxes, passing under the giant sphinx centerpiece, and enter through doors with carvings from tombs. Once registered, guests travel by boat along a river to the elevators which climb the pyramid at a 39-degree angle. The obelisk outside projects a laser light show into the central atrium of the pyramid. The apex of the pyramid contains a laser light that shoots straight up to the stars, a reference to the reverence that the Egyptians had for their heavenly gods. This laser beam is so powerful that it is one of only two earthly features that can be seen by orbiting spacecraft. The MGM Grand Las Vegas is the largest hotel and casino in the world. An 88-foot abstract reproduction of the symbolic MGM lion serves as the entryway to this complex. Humans are dwarfed by the scale of this gargantuan figure, molded of abstract planes of concrete painted a golden color. A series of smaller lions cap pilasters on the adjacent parking structure.

Abacus

The flat area at the top of a capital, dividing a column from its entablature. It usually consists of a square block, or enriched with moldings. In some orders the sides are hollowed and the angles at the corner are truncated.

Abutment

A masonry mass, pier, or solid part of a wall that takes the lateral thrust of an arch.

Acanthus

A common plant of the Mediterranean, whose leaves, stylized, form the characteristic decoration of capitals of the Corinthian and Composite orders. In scroll form it appears on friezes and panels.

Acroteria

A pedestal for statues and other ornaments placed on the apex and the lower angles of a pediment; or often refers to the ornament itself.

Agraffe

The keystone of an arch, especially when carved with a cartouche or human face.

Angle column

A free-standing or engaged column placed at the corner of a building or portico.

Anta

A pier or pilaster formed by a thickening at the end of a wall, most often used on the side of a doorway or beyond the face of an end wall.

Applied trim

Supplementary and separate decorative strips of wood or moldings applied to the face or sides of a frame.

Applique

An accessory decorative feature applied to a structure. In ornamental work, one material affixed to another.

Arabesque

Generic term for intricate and subtle surface decoration based on a mixture of geometrical patterns and botanical forms.

Arcade

A line of arches along one or both sides, supported by pillars or columns, either as free-standing or attached to a building. Applies to a line of arches fronting shops, and covered with a steel and glass skylight, usually running the length of the arcade.

Arch

A basic architectural structure built over an opening, made up of wedge-shaped blocks, supported from the sides only, the downward pressure being transformed into a lateral thrust.

Architrave

The lowest of the three divisions of a classical entablature, the main beam spanning from column to column, resting directly on the capitals.

Archivault

The ornamental molding running around the exterior curve of an arch, around the openings of windows, doors, and other openings.

Atrium

The forecourt of an early Christian basilica, with colonnades on all four sides, and usually a fountain in the center. It was derived from the entrance court of a Roman dwelling.

Attic

A low wall or story above the cornice of a classical facade; originally, a small top story.

Balcony

A projecting platform, usually on the exterior of a building, sometimes supported from below, sometimes cantilevered, enclosed with a railing, balustrade, or other vertical parapet.

Baluster

One of a number of short vertical members used to support a stair railing.

Baluster column

A short, thick-set column in a subordinate position, as in the windows of early Italian Renaissance facades.

Balustrade

An entire railing system, as along the edge of a balcony, including a top rail, bottom rail and balusters.

Band

A flat horizontal fascia, or a continuous member or series of moldings projecting slightly from the wall plane, encircling a building or along a wall, that makes a division in the wall.

Banded rustication

Alternating smooth ashlar and roughly textured stone.

Banding

Horizontal subdivisions of a column or wall using profile or material change.

Bargeboard

A trim board used on the edge of gables where the roof extends over the wall; it either covers the rafter or occupies the place of a rafter.

Barrel vault

A masonry vault resting on two parallel walls having the form of a half cylinder; sometimes called a tunnel vault.

Base

The lowest part of a building, pillar or wall.

Bas-relief

Sculptural decoration in low relief, in which none of the figures or motifs are separated from their background, projecting less than half their true proportions from the wall or surface.

Batter

A wall that is gently sloping inward towards the top.

Bay

A principal compartment or division in the architectural arrangement of a building, marked either by buttresses or pilasters in the wall, by the disposition of the main arches and pillars, or by any repeated spatial units that separate it into corresponding portions.

Bay window

A window forming a recess in a room and projecting outwards from the wall either in a rectangular, polygonal or semi-circular form. Some are supported on corbels or on projecting moldings.

Beltcourse

A projecting horizontal course of masonry, of the same or dissimilar material used to throw off water from the wall; usually coincides with the edge of an interior floor.

Bezant

An ornament shaped like a coin or disc.

Blind Arch

An arch within a wall that contains a recessed flat wall rather than framing an opening. Used to enrich an otherwise unrelieved expanse of masonry.

Board and Batten

A form of sheathing for wood frame buildings consisting of wide boards, usually placed vertically, whose joints are covered by narrow strips of wood over joints or cracks.

Bond

A system of overlapping rows or courses of stones or bricks used to provide stability and strength in the construction of walls. There are a large number of standard patterns.

Bracket

A projection from a vertical surface providing structural or visual support under cornices, balconies, windows, or any other overhanging member.

Bridge

A structure which spans a depression or provides a passage between two points at a height above the ground affording passage for pedestrians and vehicles. A footbridge is a narrow structure designed to carry pedestrians only.

Buttress

An exterior mass of masonry projecting from the wall to create additional strength and support, absorbing the lateral thrusts from roof vaults.

Canopy

A flat, simple, molded shelf-like projection above the door or window, perhaps displaying brackets or consoles to support them.

Cantilever

A structural member or any other element projecting beyond its supporting wall or column and weighted at one end to carry a proportionate weight on the projecting end.

Capital

The upper member of a column, pillar, pier or pilaster. It is usually decorated. It may carry an architrave, arcade or impost block.

Cartouche

A decorative ornamental tablet resembling a scroll of paper with the center either inscribed or left plain, but framed with an elaborate scroll-like carving.

Caryatid

A name given to a draped statue of the female figure, first used as supporting members instead of columns in Greek architecture, as at the Erectheum at the Acropolis.

Casement

A window pivoted on its side, like the pages of a book, and usually taller than it is wide.

Casing

A trim member, molding, framing or lining around door and window openings which give a finished appearance. They may be flat or molded.

Castellation

A notched or indented parapet, originally used for fortifications, but afterwards used on church facades and was intended as ornament.

Ceiling

The undercovering of a roof, or floor, generally concealing the structural members from the room below, or the underside surface of vaulting.

Centering

A temporary support placed under vaults and arches to sustain them while under construction, usually by a wooden framework.

Chamfer

The groove or oblique surface made when an edge or corner is beveled or cut away, usually at a 45 degree angle.

Chimney

A noncombustible structure containing one or more flues, serving a fireplace.

Clerestory

An upper story or row of windows rising above the adjoining parts of the building, designed as a means of admitting increased light into the inner space of the building.

Clocktower

Any instrument for measuring or indicating time, such as a mechanical device with a numbered dial and moving hands or pointers positioned in a single tower, or a tower-like portion of a structure.

Cloister

A square court surrounded by an open arcade, a covered walk around a courtyard, or the whole courtyard.

Clustered column

A column or pillar composed of a cluster of attached or semi-attatched additional shafts, grouped together to act as a single structural element.

Coffer

A recessed boxlike panel in a ceiling or vault, usually square, but often octagonal or lozenge shaped, sometimes dressed with simple moldings or elaborately ornamented.

Colonnade

A combination or grouping of columns paced at regular intervals, and arranged with regard to their structural or ornamental relationship to the building. They can be aligned either straight or arced in a circular pattern.

Column

A vertical structural compression member or shaft supporting a load which acts in the direction of its vertical axis and has both a base and a capital, designed to support an entablature or balcony.

Column Baseplate

A horizontal plate beneath the bottom of a column which transmits and distributes the column load to the supporting materials below the plate.

Composite Capital

One of the five classical orders which combines acanthus leaves of the Corinthian with the volutes of the Ionic.

Conservatory

A glass-enclosed room in a house, originally for the cultivation of plants, now including rooms as solariums.

Console

A vertical decorative bracket in the form of a scroll, projecting from a wall to support a cornice, window, or a piece of sculpture.

Coping

A protective covering over the top course of a wall or parapet, either flat or sloping on the upper surface to throw off water. If it extends beyond the wall it may be cut with a drip to protect the wall below.

Corbel

In masonry construction, a row of brick projected further outward as it rises to support a cornice.

Corbel Table

A projecting course of masonry supported on corbels near the top of a wall, as a parapet or cornice.

Corinthian Order

The most ornamental of the three orders of architecture used by the Greeks, characterized by a high base, pedestal, slender fluted shaft with fillets, ornate capitals using stylized acanthus leaves, and an elaborate cornice.

Corner

The position at which two lines or surfaces meet. The immediate exterior of the angle formed by the two lines or surfaces, as a corner of a building or structure.

Cornerstone

A stone that is situated at a corner of a building uniting two intersecting walls, usually located near the base, and often carrying information about the structure.

Cornice

A projecting shelf along the top of a wall supported by ornamental brackets or a series of consoles.

Coupled Column

Columns set as close pairs with a wider space between the pairs.

Course

A layer of masonry units running horizontally in a wall or over an arch, bonded with mortar. The horizontal joints run the entire length; the vertical joints are broken so that no two form a continuous line.

Court

An open space about which a building or several buildings are grouped, completely or partially enclosing the space. They may be roofed over with glass or open to the air.

Courtyard

An open area within the confines of other structures, sometimes as a semi-public space.

Crenellation

A pattern of repeated depressed openings in a fortification wall.

Cupola

A tower-like device rising from the roof, usually terminating in a miniature dome or turret with a lantern or windows to let light in.

Curtain wall

A method of construction in which all building loads are transmitted to a metal skeleton frame, so that the non-bearing exterior walls of metal and glass are simply a protective cladding.

Dentil

An ornamental block resembling teeth, used as moldings often in continuous bands just below the cornice.

Dome

A curved roof structure that spans an area on a circular base, often hemispherical. A section can be semicircular, pointed or segmented.

Door

A hinged, sliding, tilting, or folding panel for closing openings in a wall or at entrances to buildings.

Door Surround

An ornamental border encircling the sides and top of a door frame.

Doorway

The framework in which the door hangs, or the entrance to a building.

Doric Order

First and simplest of the Greek orders, consisting of relatively short shafts meeting with a sharp arris, simple capital and square abacus.

Dormer

A structure projecting from a sloping roof usually housing a vertical window placed in a small gable or in a ventilating louver.

Downspout

A vertical pipe that carrys water from the roof gutters to the ground or cistern.

Dressing

Masonry and moldings of better quality than the facing materials, used around openings or at corners of buildings.

Eave

The projecting overhang at the lower edge of a roof that sheds rain water.

Elevator

A platform or enclosure that can be raised or lowered in a vertical shaft that transports people or freight.

Engaged Column

A column that is attached to and appears to emerge from the wall, as decoration or as a structural buttress.

Entablature

The superstructure which lies above the columns in the architrave (immediately above the column), frieze (central part), and cornice (upper projecting moldings).

Entasis

Intentional slight curvature given to the profile of a column to correct the optical illusion that it is thinner in the middle.

Entrance

Any passage that affords entry into a building; an exterior door, vestibule or lobby.

Escalator

A moving stairway consisting of steps attached to an inclined continuously moving belt for transporting passengers up or down between the floors in a structure.

Facade

The main exterior face of a building, particularly one of its main sides, almost always containing an entrance and characterized by an elaboration of stylistic details.

Fanlight

A semicircular window, usually over a door with radiating bars suggesting an open fan.

Fascia

A broad horizontal member or molding with nominal thickness, projecting from the wall.

Fenestration

The design and placement of windows in a building.

Festoon

Hanging clusters of fruit, tied in a bunch with leaves and flowers; used as decoration on pilasters and panels, usually hung between rosettes and skulls of animals.

Finial

An ornament at the top of a spire, pinnacle or gable which acts as a terminal

Flush Bead

An insert bead or convex molding, with its outer surface flush with adjacent surfaces.

Fluting

The hollows or parallel channels cut vertically in the shape of columns, pilasters and piers. Some are separated by a sharp edge or arris, some by a small fillet.

Fountain

An architectural setting incorporating a continuous or artificial water supply, fed by a system of pipes and nozzles through which water is forced under pressure to produce a stream of ornamental jets.

Fractable

A coping on the gable end of a building when carried above the roof, and broken into steps or curves forming an ornamental outline.

Fretting

Decoration produced by cutting away the background of a pattern in stone or wood leaving the rest as grating.

Frieze

An elevated horizontal continuous band or panel, usually located below the cornice.

Gable

The entire triangular end of a wall, above the level of the eaves, the top of which conforms to the slope of the roof which abuts against it, sometimes stepped and sometimes curved in a scroll shape.

Gargoyle

A spout carrying water from the roof and frequently carved with grotesque figures or animals with open mouths from which the water springs.

Gateway

A structure at an entrance gate, or a passageway through a wall.

Gazebo

A fanciful small structure, used as a summer house that is usually octagonal in plan with a steeply pitched roof that is topped by a finial. The sides are usually open, or latticed.

Gibbs Surround

The surrounding trim of a doorway or window, consisting of alternating large and small blocks of stone, like quoins. These are often connected with a narrow raised band along the face of the door, window, or arch.

Gingerbread

The highly decorative woodwork applied to a Victorian style house.

Grille

An ornamental arrangement of bars to form a screen or partition, usually of metal, wood, stone, or concrete, to cover, conceal, decorate, or protect an opening .

Groin

The curved area formed by the intersection of two vaults.

Guilloche

An ornament in the form of two or more bands twisted together in a continuous series, leaving circular openings which are filled with round ornaments.

Gutta

A small ornament resembling a droplet used under the triglyph or the cornice in Classical architecture.

Gutter

A shallow channel of metal or wood at the edge of a roof eave to catch and drain water into a downspout.

Haunch

The middle part of an arch, between the springing point and the crown.

Hood

A projection above an opening, such as a door or window serving as a screen or as protection against the weather.

Impost

The horizontal molding or capital on top of a pilaster, pier, or corbel which receives and distributes the thrust at the end of an arch.

Intaglio

Incised carving in which the forms are hollowed out of the surface; the relief in reverse, often used as a mold.

Intercolumniation

The spacing of the columns according to a system of proportions used in Classical architecture, based on the diameter of the column as the governing module.

Interfenestration

The space between the windows in a facade.

Interlaced Arches

Arches, usually circular, so constructed that their forms intersect each other.

Interlaced Ornament

A band of ornamental figures that are overlapped or intertwined to create resultant forms.

Ionic Order

An order of architecture invented by the Greeks, distinguished by an elegantly molded base, tall slender shafts with flutes separated by fillets, and capitals using the spiral volute.

Jamb

The side of a window, door, chimney, or any other vertical opening.

Jamb shaft

A small shaft having a capital and a base, placed against the jamb of a door or window.

Joint

The space between the stones or bricks in masonry or brickwork.

Keystone

The central stone or voissor at the top of the arch, the last part to be put into position to lock the arch in place, often embellished.

Kneestone
A stone which is sloped on top and flat on the bottom that supports inclined coping on the side of a gable, or a stone that breaks the horizontal joint pattern to begin the curve of an arch.

Lantern
A tower or small turret with windows, crowning a dome or cupola.

Lean-to
A shed or building having a single pitched roof, with its apex against an adjoining wall or building.

Lintel
The horizontal beam that forms the upper structural member of an opening for a window or door and supports part of the structure above it.

Loggia
A covered gallery or portico, having a colonnade on one or more sides, open to the air.

Louver
A window opening made of overlapping boards to ventilate without letting in the rain.

Lunette
A semicircular window or wall panel framed by an arch or vault.

Machicolation
Openings formed by setting the parapets out on corbels so as to project beyond the face of the wall.

Mansard Roof
A roof with a steep lower slope and a flatter upper slope on all sides, either of convex or concave shape.

Margin Draft
A narrow dressed border along the edge of a squared stone, usually the width of a chisel, as a border surrounding the rough central portion.

Medallion
An ornamental plaque with an object in relief, applied to a wall or frieze.

Minaret
The tall slender tower of a mosque from which followers are called to prayer.

Miter
The line formed by the meeting of moldings or other surfaces which intersect each other at an angle; each member is cut at half the angle of the junction.

Module
A simple ratio by which all parts of a building are related as part of an ordered system.

Molding
A decorative profile given to architectural members and subordinate parts of buildings, whether cavities or projections, such as cornices, bases, or door and window jambs and heads.

Mullion
A dividing piece between the lights of windows, taking on the characteristics of the style of the building.

Niche
A recess in a wall, usually semi-circular at the back, terminating in a half-dome, or with small pediments supported on consoles; most often used as a place for a statue.

Obelisk
A four-sided stone shaft, either monolithic or jointed, tapering to a pyramidal top.

Ogee
A double curve resembling an "S" in shape, formed by the union of a convex and concave line.

Ornament
Anything that embellishes, decorates, or adorns a structure, whether used intentionally and integrated into the structure, or applied for the sake of enhancing the buildings' form and appearance.

Overhang
The horizontal distance that the upper story or roof projects beyond the story immediately below.

Ovolo
A common convex molding usually consisting of a quarter circle in section.

Parapet
A low protective wall or railing along the edge of a roof, balcony, or similar structure.

Pargeting
A decorative feature in which flat wet plaster is ornamented by patterns either scratched or molded into it.

Panel
A portion of a flat surface recessed below the surrounding area, set off by moldings or some other distinctive feature.

Parapet
A low protective wall or railing along the edge of a raised platform, terrace, bridge, roof, balcony, and above cornices.

Pavilion
An open structure or a small ornamental building as an adjunct of a larger building.

Pedestal
A support for a column, urn, or statue, consisting of a base and a cap or cornice.

Pediment
A low-pitched triangular gable above a facade, or a smaller version over porticos above the door or window.

Pendant
A hanging ornament or suspended feature on ceilings or vaults.

Pendentive
The curved triangular surface that results when the the top corner of a square space is vaulted so as to provide a circular base for a dome.

Peristyle
A row of columns around the outside of a building or around the inside of a courtyard.

Picture Window
A large fixed pane of glass, often between two narrower operable windows, usually located to present the most attractive view to the exterior.

Pier
A free-standing support for an arch, usually composite in section and thicker than a column, but performing the same function; also, a thickened part of a wall to provide lateral support or take concentrated loads.

Pilaster
A partial pier or column, often with a base and capital that is embedded in a flat wall and projects slightly.

Pillar

A column or post supporting an arch or other superimposed load.

Pinnacle

An apex or small turret that usually tapers towards the top as a termination to a buttress.

Plinth Block

The base of a pillar, column, pedestal or statue.

Portal

An entrance, gate, or door to a building or courtyard, often decorated.

Portico

A range of columns in front of a building, often merged into the facade, including a covered walkway of which one or more sides are open.

Quoin

One of a series of stones or bricks used to mark the exterior corners of a building often through a contrast of size, shape, color or material.

Reticulated Work

Masonry constructed with diamond-shaped stones, or square stones placed diagonally or crossing in a network.

Relief

Carved or embossed decoration, raised above a background plane.

Reveal

The visible side of an opening for a window or doorway between the framework and outer surface of the wall.

Rib

A narrow projecting band on a ceiling or vault, usually structural, but sometimes decorative.

Ridgebeam

A horizontal beam at the upper edge of the rafters, below the ridge of the roof.

Roof

The external covering on the top of a building, usually of wood shingles, slates, or tiles on pitched slopes, or a variety of built-up membranes for flat roofs.

Rustication

Masonry cut in huge blocks with the surface left rough and unfinished and set with deep recessed joints, used mainly on the lower part to create the appearance of strength.

Rustic Work

In ashlar masonry the joints are grooved or channeled to render them more conspicuous; sometimes only the horizontal joints are treated in this manner.

Scroll

An ornamental molding consisting of a spiral design; or a terminal like the volutes of the Ionic capital or the "S" curves on consoles.

Section

The representation of a building or portion thereof, cut vertically at some imagined plane, so as to show the interior of the space or the profile of the member.

Shaft

The main body of a column, pilaster or pier between the capital and the base, or a thin vertical member attached to a wall or pier, often supporting an arch or vaulting rib.

Sill

The horizontal exterior member at the bottom of a window or door opening, usually sloped away from the bottom of the window for drainage of water, and overhanging the wall below.

Skewback

The sloping surface of a member which receives the component materials of an arch.

Skylight

An opening in a roof which is glazed with a transparent or translucent material used to admit natural or diffused light to the space below.

Soffit

A ceiling or exposed underside surface of entablatures, archways, balconies, beams, lintels or columns.

Space Frame

A three-dimensional structural framework made up of interconnected triangular elements that enclose a space; as opposed to a frame where all the elements lie in a single plane.

Spandrel

The triangular space formed between the sides of adjacent arches and the line across their tops. In a skeletal frame building it consists of the walls inside the columns and between the top of the window of one story and the sill of the window above.

Spire

The tapering roof of a tower.

Springer

The impost or place where the vertical support for an arch terminates and the curve of the arch begins.

Stair

A series of steps or flights connected by landings, which permit passage between two or more levels.

Steel Frame

A skeleton of steel beams and columns providing all that is structurally necessary for the building to stand.

Step

A stair unit which consists of one tread and one riser.

Surround

An encircling border or decorative frame around a door, window or other opening.

Table

Applied generally to all horizontal bands of moldings, base moldings and cornices.

Terminus

A bust or figure of the upper part of the human body terminated in a plain rectangular block, sometimes attached to a wall as a pillar, or springing out of a column.

Tower

A tall structure designed for observation, communication or defense. A bell tower is synonomous with "campanile" and church towers were for hanging bells, hence "belfry."

Trabeation

Construction using upright posts and horizontal beams and lintels, rather than arches or vaults.

Truss

A composite structural system composed of straight members transmitting stress along each member, joined with hinges to form triangles.

Tympanum

The triangular space between the horizontal and sloping cornices, immediately above the opening of a doorway.

Vault

An arched roof in a continuous semicircular ceiling that extends in a straight line.

Veneer

The covering of one material with thin slices of another to give an effect of greater richness.

Veranda

Similar to a balcony but located on the ground level; It can extend around one, two or all sides of a building.

Vestibule

An intermediate chamber or passage located between the entrance and interior or court of a building, that serves as a shelter or transitional element from exterior to interior space.

Volute

A spiral ornament characteristic of Ionic capitals; a scroll.

Voussoir

A wedge-shaped block whose converging sides radiate from the center forming an element of an arch or vaulted ceiling.

Wall

A structure which encloses or subdivides a space with a continuous surface, except where fenestration or other openings occur.

Water Table

A horizontal offset in a wall sloped on the top to throw off the water.

Weathering

A slight inclination given to the surface of horizontal joints in masonry construction to prevent water from collecting in channels, or flutes separated by two narrow flat spaces, occurring over the center of columns.

Window

An exterior wall opening, usually glazed, admitting light and air, fitted with the assembly of window frame, glazing, and operable elements. These operable windows are identified by the way they work; double hung, casement, sliding, pivoting, and louvered.

Window Head

The upper horizontal cross member or decorative element of a window frame.

Ziggurat

A temple tower having the form of a stepped or terraced pyramid or successively receeding stories.

PRECEDENTS

HISTORICAL FACADES WORLDWIDE
2 - 48, 50 - 69 Photos by the author
49 (bottom) Photo by Hans-Christian Lischewski

ORNAMENT

74 - 114
ORNAMENTAL DETAILS ON BUILDING FACADES
Photos by the author

115
DOORKNOCKERS
Photographer: Joy Arnold

116 - 181
Photos by the author

RENOVATION

183
Title Page
Photographer: James W. Rhodes / Beyer Blinder Belle

186 - 189
FACADE
Photos by the author from the 1960 portfolio
FACADE: The Changing Face of a City

190 - 191
BROOKLYN MUSEUM SCULPTURE GARDEN
Photos by the author

192
ART CENTER PROJECT
Photos by the author

193
RESTORATION OF THE HIGHWAY TABERNACLE CHURCH
Philadelphia, PA.
Wiss, Janney, Elstner Associates, Inc.
Princeton, NJ
Project Manager: Andrew Osborn
Photographer: Gary McKinnis

194 - 195
SCAFFOLDING / SIDEWALK BRIDGES
Photos by the author

196
THE CARNEGIE: RESTORATION AND RENOVATION
Pittsburgh, PA
Williams Trebilcock Whitehead, Architects
Pittsburgh, PA
Photographer: Robert P. Rushak

197
LOUVRE
Paris, France
Photos by the author

197
FLATIRON BUILDING
Photos by the author

198 - 199
THE GUARANTY BUILDING
Buffalo, N.Y.
Cannon: Restoration Architects for Adler & Sullivan
Grand Island, N.Y.
Photographer: Patricia Layman Bazelon

200 - 203
SMALL-SCALE RESTORATIONS / COMMERCIAL RENOVATIONS
Photos by the author

204
ERIE COMMUNITY COLLEGE - CITY CAMPUS
Erie, PA.
Cannon - Restoration and Adaptive re-use of James Knox Taylor Post Office and Federal Building
Erie, PA.
Photographer: Patricia Layman Bazelon

205
ROCHESTER CITY HALL
Photos by the author

206
BLEECKER COURT
New York City
Avinosh K. Malhotra Architects
New York City
Photographer: Julian Olivas

207
MARSH AND MCLENNAN BUILDING
Baltimore, MD
RTKL Associates, Inc.
Baltimore, MD
Photographer: Scott McDonald / Hedrich Blessing

208 - 209
CIRCLE CENTRE MALL
Indianapolis, IN
Centre Venture Associates, a Joint Venture of
CSO / Architects, Inc. Brown Day Mullins Dierdorf (BDMD)
Design Architects: Ehrenkrantz and Ekstut
Project Directors: Dave Halvorson (CSO) / Greg Jacoby (BDMD)
Project Managers: Sam F. Miller, AIA (CSO) / Lois Morales (BDMD)
Indianapolis, IN
Photos: Courtesy of Sam F. Miller, AIA

210
COMBINED FACILITY
New York City
The Stein Partnership
New York City
Photography: The Stein Partnership

211
THE RECONSTRUCTION OF SHEPARD HALL EXTERIOR , CCNY
New York City
The Stein Partnership
New York City
Photography: The Stein Partnership

212 - 213
COLISEUM THEATER ADAPTIVE RE-USE / BANANA REPUBLIC
Seattle, WA
Shell and core rehabilitation architect: NBBJ
Seattle, WA
James Adams, Principal / Craig Hardman, Project Manager /
Robert Lane, Project Architect / Walt Reiner, Technical Architect /
Ed Storer, Specifications
Photography: Fred Housel

214
MELLON CENTER (The Union Trust Building)
Pittsburgh, PA
Burt Hill /Kosar Rittlemann
Pittsburgh, PA
Photographer: Hedrich - Blessing

214
MELLON INDEPENDENCE CENTER
Pittsburgh, PA
Burt Hill Kosar Rittlemen
Philadelphia, PA
Photography: Hedrich - Blessing

215
St. REGIS HOTEL
New York City
Brennan Beer Gorman Monk / Interiors
New York City
Photographer: Anthony P. Albarello

215
ESSEX HOUSE NIKKO HOTEL
New York City
Brennan Beer Gorman / Architects
New York City
Photographer: Peter Vitale

216 - 217
RESTORATION AND ADAPTIVE USE OF FLEET BANK CORPORATE
HEADQUARTERS
Albany, N.Y.
Einhorn Yaffee Prescott Architects
Albany, N.Y.
Photography: Exterior and interiors, William Murphy

218
MUSEUM CENTER AT CINCINNATI UNION TERMINAL
Cincinnati, OH
Glaser Associates
Design Architects: E. Verner Johnson & Associates
Cincinnati, OH
Photographer: Robert Ames Cook

219
ORSAY MUSEUM
Paris, France
Photos by the author

220
799 MARKET STREET
San Francisco, CA
Gensler and Associates
San Francisco, CA
Photographer: David Wakely

220
MASONIC BUILDING
Denver, CO
Gensler and Associates
Architectural Renovation / Restoration
San Francisco, CA
Photographer: Ed LaCasse

RENEWAL

259
ARCH OF DEFENSE
Photos by the author

260
YOHGA PROJECT
Tokyo, Japan
Callison Architecture
Seattle, WA
Rendering: Andrew West

261
E WALK on the New 42nd Street
New York City
Tishman Urban Development Corporation,
a unit of Tishman Realty & Construction Co., Inc.
Hotel design: Arquitectonica, Miami FL
Entertainment/retail design: D'Agostino Izzo Quirk
Photographer: Tishman Urban Development Corp. / Roy Wright

262
DOLPHIN AND SWAN HOTELS
Orlando, FL
Michael Graves
Princeton, NJ
Photos by the author

263
LUXOR / MGM GRAND HOTEL
Las Vegas
Photos by the author